MW01231765

© 2018 Frank J. Antonucci

All rights reserved.

ISBN: 1986559440
ISBN 13: 9781986559447
Library of Congress Control Number: 2017905660
LCCN Imprint Name:
CreateSpace Independent Publishing Platform
North Charleston, South Carolina

This book is dedicated to my loving wife of forty-six years Christine, whose continued support gave me the confidence I needed in succeeding and reaching my goals.

Love Always, Frank

Table of Contents

TABLE OF CONTENTS...0
GROWING UP ITALIAN 1
My Parents 8
I am Born..11
Delivering Chickens..11
Dad's Helper 12
Moving to Saint Clair Shores..............................14
First Grade at Wheat Elementary.......................15
Parochial School 16
Detroit News Paper Route 17
Vincent..20
My passion for cars...25
1956 Ford Fairlane Victoria 28
Customizing My Dad's New Ford 33
Experiencing Grown-Up's Words 35
Ottawa Junior High..36
John F. Kennedy...39
Developing My Identity.......................................40
Lakeview High School 43
Algebra Class 43
Our Family Had Grown 46
D&W Standard Service.......................................50
My 1964 Galaxy 500 54
Detroit Autorama 61
Plymouth Troubleshooting Contest 68
Would I Graduate?..72
Saying Good-By to D&W.....................................78
Recommendations and Decisions 80
The Detroit Riots and Vietnam 90
Enlisting in the Army National Guard 92
Readjusting to Civilian Life................................100
Starting Over 103
College, the Second Time Around 107
Christine 109
BECOMING A MAN 111
Preparing for the Wedding.................................111
My New Job at the Dealership............................117
National Body Repair 119
BACK TO SCHOOL..130
The New Teacher 130
Meeting the Class..134

Classroom Strategies 137
Mr. Bully...147
The C Group 150
Meetings…Too Late 153
Ronnie...154
Summertime at the Lincoln Dealer 158
Teaching, Year Two..161
Students Manipulating the System..165
Second Year Meet and Greet..168
The Five-Hundred-Point Scale 168
Developing a Connection..172
Hands-On Learning Styles 174
They Will Never Forget...177
The Program Keeps Going...182
Growing with my Class 183
My Life Changed Forever..190
My New Assignment 202
More Changes in My Future..209
Tuesday, September 11, 2001...221
The Cousino Parking Lot..222
Football...225
Another Assignment 226
Principal and Director: The Final Chapter............................229
Home Again..230
The Students Meet Us...234
Update Time 241
The Team...245
The Counselor Julie..248
Meeting in My Office..257
First Appearances...259
Infusing Academics into Hands-On Learning............................267
Student Awards and Recognition 270
Remodeling...272
A New Governor 274

Acknowledgments

I would like to express my very great appreciation to Diane Russell and Julie Sayers for their valuable and constructive suggestions during the writing of this book. The willingness to give their time so generously has been very much appreciated.

I want to thank the following people who have made a positive impact in my life:
My dad
Frank Sirianni
Frank Mini Sr.
Ken Wall
Ray Dixon
Sue L. Nye
Joseph G. Sayers
Dr. Jay Inwald
Robert L. Koskodan
Alfred F. Bracciano
Pastor Joseph Tabbi
Sister Eileen Rice

Being Cool through the eyes of my 10 year old grandson

Salvatore

Forward

Frank Antonucci has a story to tell. A life story of struggle and heartbreak; a story of success and great joy. When I was asked to write a forward for his book I was so pleased, because I knew that through the candid story telling of his own life he would continue to inspire others and help readers evaluate their place in life and go forward.

I have had the pleasure of knowing Frank during his career as an educator and mentor and have been able to witness the positive changes he has made in his students, family, friends and peers. Working alongside Frank has been one of the great experiences of my life. He has inspired me personally to embrace my strengths and attempt things that I would have never believed I could. He has the ability to inspire, encourage and motivate others; to make them be the best they can be.

Frank has had success as a son, husband, father, friend and educator. Yet, his success did not come without great personal struggle. He learned being successful in life does not mean being successful in school. Instead he took a passion and a skill and made it his path to success. Frank Antonucci is a testimony to what a person can accomplish. He turned his love of hands on learning and his passion for cars into this, his life story. He sustained setbacks and a debilitating accident, but relied on his God given strengths to conquer obstacles in his way.

Beginning with his early schooling and family relationships, and up through his retirement as a successful and loved educator, Frank had to make many choices. All of them were not the best, but all of them were learning and growing experiences. This book will help others to do the same. He is a man of undeniable integrity and dignity, hopefully as you read this book, his experience will change your life. If you are one of Frank's students, family, friends or peers, you will understand and appreciate his story. If not…you are in for a treat! It is a joy to call him my friend, work with him and love him.

Enjoy!

Suzanne Nye

My hope is that sharing my life's journey of successes and failures will give you inspiration to reach for and obtain your ultimate goal of success.

Growing Up Italian

My father (Joseph Peter) and mother (Rose Angela) were born here in the United States and were proud Italian Americans. I am the second oldest of seven children. I have four sisters and two brothers.

My father's mother (Petrina) and her husband (Francis) were both born in San Pier Niceto, on the island of Sicily. San Pier Niceto is a *comune* (a township) in the province of Messina on the island of Sicily, located about 170 kilometers east of Palermo and about 20 kilometers west of Messina. As of December 31, 2004, it had a population of 3,084 and an area of 36.3 square kilometers. Although I have never visited Sicily, I have seen many pictures of the breathtaking scenery. Sicily is one of the best places in the region to grow artichokes, olives, and tomatoes, and the list could go on and on. This is the result of very fertile soil. I can visualize the rolling mountains and the scent of the ripe olives and blossoming grapes ready to be harvested.

My mother's father (Samuel) was born in Grotte, a small village in Sicily. Grotte is a comune in the province of Agrigento, located about eighty kilometers southeast of Palermo and about fourteen kilometers northeast of Agrigento. Her mother (MaryAnn) was born in Reggio di Calabria. Calabria is in the southernmost part of Italy. Reggio di Calabria is commonly known as Reggio Calabria or simply Reggio. It is the biggest city and the capital of the province of Reggio Calabria and the seat of the regional council of Calabria.

It is not uncommon to be asked by other Italian Americans where your parents come from. My response was always that my mother was from Calabria and that my dad was from Sicily. Some would refer to me as a "Siciliano", and others would say, "No, he's Calabrese," almost in a humorous way (referring to the town in Italy where my ancestors came from).

Sicilians are often thought of as having strong and stubborn personalities. The Calabrese were commonly known as *testa duras*, which, when translated into English, means hardheaded and difficult to reason with. Their way is the only way. Who, me? The Sicilians...well, let's just say if you were from Sicily, you were a made man or were being made an offer you couldn't refuse. You know what I mean?

My dad's father, Francis, passed away when my dad was two years old. In those days, the cause of death sometimes was not clear. Some said he died in a car accident, and others said he died of a coal miner's disease known as black lung. I am not sure how he died, but I would have liked to meet him. I was named after him.

My dad's mother, Petrina, remained a single mother with three children for the next six years. My dad was the middle child and the only boy in the family. He had an older sister, Frances, and a younger sister, Patricia. At that time, they lived in Albany, New York. Approximately six years following the death of her husband, Petrina moved her family to Punxsutawney, Pennsylvania, where my father attended school. However, back in the day, raising a family on one income was difficult. The women stayed home, and the men went to work.

When dad completed the eighth grade at the age of thirteen, he had to quit school and provide for his mother and two sisters. He worked at many types of odd jobs: delivering groceries, lawn work, handyman repairs, and working at the local automotive repair shop. When he turned sixteen, he enrolled in barber school and became a barber. He signed up for the US Navy at the end of World War II, and his tour of duty consisted of being the head barber on a ship. My dad was fortunate not to see or experience any combat duty. Meanwhile, back at home in Pennsylvania, Grandma met and married a widower named Joseph Sano. He also had two children from his previous marriage. Joseph Sano was a coal miner for twenty-four years and spoke very little English. Coal mining was not the greatest occupation. It was very dangerous and hazardous work. At the end of World War II, the word spread that there were plenty of manufacturing jobs available in the automotive industry—up north in the city of Detroit, Michigan.

At the end of the 1940s, the Sano family decided to move north so that Joseph and my father could pursue careers in the automotive industry. There was a relatively new car company named the Hudson Motor Car Company, located on the corner of Jefferson and Conner in Detroit. Today all that remains there is the shell of the once-great car manufacturer.[1] A man could make excellent pay working on the assembly line—approximately three to four dollars per day,[2] and you didn't have to breathe hazardous coal dust. After my dad was honorably discharged from the navy, he also worked at the Hudson Motor Car Company.

---

[1] The Hudson Motor Car company made Hudson and other brand automobiles in Detroit from 1909 to 1954. In 1954, Hudson merged with the Nash-Kelvinator Corporation to form American Motors (AMC). The Hudson name was continued through the 1957 model year, after which it was discontinued.
[2] According to the February 2, 1947, issue of *LIFE*.

After settling in Detroit, Grandpa Sano did what he loved to do best—grow a garden. He was a master at growing vegetables and fruit trees. I remember when I would visit him, I'd ask my grandma, "Where's Grandpa?"

Her response would always be to point to his garden.

"Hello, Grandpa," I would say, and he would smile and nod his head. He was paying close attention to ensure that all of the rich black soil was raked uniformly and that there were no weeds interfering with the growth of his vegetables. I stood silently watching him rake, weed, and water his garden. He appeared to be in an intense trance, almost as if he were talking to his vegetables and did not want to be interrupted. I kept silent, just watching him and waiting. He enjoyed picking the vegetables and bringing them in for Grandma to prepare for dinner. He'd carefully pick each vegetable, one by one, and place it in his old wooden basket. He washed them off carefully, as if he didn't want to bruise or damage his prize vegetables—lettuce, onions, cucumbers, and, of course, bright-red tomatoes.

I sat and watched him, and occasionally he would say something to me in Italian. I always nodded my head as if I understood what he was saying. I didn't understand a word of it. Whatever he was saying seemed to be good because he said it with a smile. One time, I thought he was asking me to get or do something for him—maybe get a rake or a shovel? I couldn't bring myself to let him know I didn't understand him, that I didn't know what he was saying, so I went to the garage and brought him a rake. He looked at me in a weird way, so I thought maybe he wanted a shovel, and therefore I brought him a shovel—wrong again.

He called me a crazy baccala. I didn't know what that meant until many years afterward. *Baccala* is the Italian word for salted codfish. In retrospect, he could have called me something other than a crazy baccala.

Oh, those childhood memories—the olden days. Visiting Grandpa and Grandma's house was a special treat for us. Grandma was different. Although she spoke only broken English, I could understand what she was saying. It was a treat for us to go into her kitchen because we knew that she was baking something good to eat. The room was warm from the oven, and the air would be filled with the aroma of her freshly baked bread or Italian cookies waiting to cool off and be eaten. Umm, good! We looked on with anticipation, waiting for her to ask us if we wanted to have a cookie or a slice of fresh hot sesame-seed bread. Before we answered her, we had to have the go-ahead from our dad. We didn't accept or say anything until we had his approval. We waited for him to nod his head yes and say, "Use your manners."

Then, Grandma would bring out the butter knives and plates, and we would eat until our stomachs were full. Umm. We spread the butter over it nice and thick and enjoyed eating her bread. We didn't know the definition of—or had ever heard the word—cholesterol. We just knew that her bread was good!

My mother came from an affluent, well-to-do family. She often reflected back to the olden days of maids, chauffeur-driven limousines, horseback riding and the finer things in life. My grandfather (Mom's father) co-owned a poultry business with his brothers, named Buscemi and Sons. They were located in the Eastern Market, which was on the

5

east side of Detroit. Grandpa B. was a kind and giving man. He may have had a tough side, but we never saw it.

He also had a green thumb and loved his garden. I remember going over to visit him, and he'd be working in the garden. It always amazed me when he'd cut a branch from one fruit tree and graft it onto another, and then the following year, it would produce fruit. He also spoke broken English, but I understood when he asked me to bring him a *shovel-a* or a *rake-a*.

He drove a 1953 Chevrolet five-window pickup truck—a collector's item in today's world.

Example of my Grandpa's 1953 five window pick-up truck
By SG2012 [CC BY-SA 2.0 (https://creativecommons.org/licenses/by-sa/2.0)]

All of my uncles and aunts and cousins would go to his house on Christmas Eve and celebrate his birthday. Italian tradition is walking through the front door and immediately kiss and hug our uncles and aunts. The aroma from the kitchen left little to my imagination.

The special dessert and baked Italian goodies covered the table in the sunroom, but none of that was to be eaten until we first ate the food Grandma B. had prepared.

I couldn't keep my eyes off those huge cooking pots full of her yummy spaghetti sauce. The heat from the oven reminded me of the hot August summer. I peeked inside the oven and saw she was cooking her famous stuffed meatballs and homemade Italian sausage. "Frankie," my mom warned, "close the oven door. You might burn yourself."

"OK, Mom." Most Italians did everything in their basement. They ate dinner, they washed the dishes, and the kids played in the basement. The upstairs was kept as a showplace for when company came to visit. The furniture was usually French provincial (very uncomfortable) and covered with clear plastic, as were the lampshades. Grandma had a beautiful dining room, but we always ate and spent time in the basement.

My grandpa always had treats for his grandchildren: Tootsie Pop suckers, and Vernors or 7-Up pop. (In Michigan, we call soda *"pop"*) He loved to do things with us and have fun. Sometimes I think he had more fun than we did. If it wasn't dunking for apples, it was removing a fifty-cent piece stuck to a frying pan with soap.

The frying pan would be hanging from a string nailed to the rafters of the basement. The object was to hold your hands behind your back and try to remove the coin with your teeth that was secured with soap on the bottom of the frying pan. The person who removed the coin kept it. Unfortunately, sometimes you also got a mouthful of soap. We laughed and cheered one another on, for we all wanted that fifty-cent coin. There were no video games back in the day, no other electronic games —just good old-fashioned creative fun. I will never forget Grandpa B's smile and thick graying hair.

Grandma B. stood about four foot zero and loved to cook. A typical Italian grandmother, her kitchen was her domain. On Sundays, when we were there for dinner, she

7

made enough food for an army, although there were only ten of us sitting at her table. Her famous words were "Eat! Eat! Don't you like Grandma's food?" A guilt trip, of course, the Italian way. She spoke broken English. She had married my grandpa when she was only fourteen years old. By today's standards, my grandpa would be in jail.

Grandma was a devoted mother of five, and she knew how to cook and bake. As the years passed, she handed down some of her recipes to my loving wife, Christine. Grandma always remembered those long-lost recipes in her head and rarely wrote anything down. Today, we'd call her a stay-at-home mom.

During the dark days of the Depression, my grandparents opened their doors and gave money and fed many who were in need. My grandparents were both generous, kind and loving people. We learned so much by the example they set for us.

My Parents

In 1945, my mother, Rose Angela Buscemi, married my father, Joseph Peter Antonucci. I often heard my parents reminisce about their extravagant and beautiful wedding. My mom's version was that it was a storybook wedding, and my dad's version reminded her how much money it cost. She came from an affluent family, and he was a poor boy from Pennsylvania. The wedding was held at the infamous[3] Book Cadillac located in the heart of downtown Detroit.

---

[3] The Purple Gang, headquartered out of the Book Cadillac Hotel in downtown Detroit, was an organized crime faction that controlled the streets of southeastern Michigan during the height of Prohibition with an iron fist.

After the wedding and honeymoon were over, my parents moved into an apartment building, one that had four separate units. We lived on a street named Fisher, on the east side of Detroit, until I was almost five years old. The house we lived in seemed like a mansion to me. It was a huge two-story upper flat, large enough to accommodate the four of us: Mom and Dad, my older sister and me. In those days, the family unit was very close. We saw our aunts, uncles, and grandparents on a regular basis. We made time for one another; families stayed and lived together. The home we lived in was purchased by my paternal grandmother. This house was large enough for our family and my dad's three sisters (Frances, Josephine, and his stepsister May) and their families. Today we would have called it an apartment house.

The neighborhood was mixed and diverse. Although prejudices existed, I was not aware of any. Oh, how nice it was to be unaware of all the differences and misconceptions, without any biases or prejudices that the adults had. If only we could be kids once again. Those days, we knew who our neighbors were. People sat on the front porches and enjoyed the comfort of their homes.

Oh, how I loved the smell of fresh air and the blossoming of the trees and flowers in the spring. We didn't have a television because only the rich owned one. Instead, we loved riding our bicycles and pulling our wagons around the long blocks. Without a care in the world, we enjoyed playing in the fresh air. When we'd go over to our next-door neighbor's house, Mrs. Thompson's, she always had some ice-cold freshly squeezed lemonade. She'd see my empty glass, but I was afraid to ask until she asked me, "Frankie, would you care for another glass?"

"Yes, Mrs. Thompson. Thank you, Mrs. Thompson." We never noticed she was black (African American), and we didn't care.

Example of Dad's 1929 Dodge
By Bob Adams from Amanzimtoti, South Africa
(1929 Dodge Brothers sedan)
*[CC BY-SA 2.0 (*__https://creativecommons.org/licenses/by-__
__sa/2.0__*)]*

Parked in the street in front of our house was my dad's 1929 Dodge sedan with real wooden-spoke wheels. I enjoyed sitting on the curb, watching him polish the wheels, one spoke at a time. He used a special wax made especially for wooden spokes. I remember the smell coming from the neighbor's barbecue grill and the kids in the neighborhood stopping by and asking me, "What is your dad doing?"

I'd say, "He is polishing the wooden wheels with a special wax." I sat there like Mr. Big. After all, I was in charge of handing him the clean polishing cloths. These days were perfect—clear and sunny, seventy degrees with a slight breeze—days I will never forget.

However, there were dark and sad moments on Fisher Street. I had a sister who was born between my oldest sister and me, and she died at the age of six months from complications from pneumonia. During the mid-1950s, doctors didn't have cures or even diagnoses for many common health issues. I often heard my mom and dad talking about their loss. I believe they never recovered from this tragic loss. I am still not sure how anyone can recover from the death of a child.

I am Born

I was born on February 26, 1950, in the city of Detroit and named Francis Joseph Antonucci. My dad told everyone how disappointed he had been when their firstborn was a girl because he really wanted her to be a boy. Then another girl – my sister who died far too early. Finally, his first son –me– was born. Many years later, he regretted what he had said about the girls, without realizing the heartaches it caused.

When I was two months old, I had to have surgery near my heart, and I never knew why until my later years. I'd had fluid building around my heart, and the surgery was invasive. I was cut halfway across my back, and I was in the hospital for a long time. Medical technology has changed immensely since 1950, thank God.

Delivering Chickens

My dad and I were inseparable. He took me everywhere he went. During the day, he often took me on his delivery route when he could. I loved sitting in the passenger seat as we went to the different poultry stores to deliver live chickens. I was Mr. Big Stuff. On many of his regular stops, the storeowners often invited us in for a sandwich or a bottle of 7-Up or Vernors pop.

On the days I couldn't go on the deliveries with my dad, he would drop me off at Grandma Sano's house. I didn't want to be separated from him and would cry as I heard the sound of his truck driving off, leaving me behind. I was angry, and couldn't understand why he wouldn't take me with him. I waited until he returned to pick me up, listened for his whistle as he walked in the door and called me, "Skippy, ready to go home?" I immediately forgot he had left me there, hugged him, and jumped into the truck. Please do not misunderstand me. I loved my Grandma S; she was great. She had a parakeet named Robin. I'd help her feed Robin and clean the cage. She also made yummy treats for me to eat. I still miss her.

Dad's Helper

Although my dad had dropped out school at an early age, he learned to develop the hands-on skills he'd been born with. I learned many things by watching dad and handing him the tools he asked for. He called me "Skip." And would say, "Skip, hand me the screwdriver. Skip, hand me the open-end wrench."

Dad worked for Grandpa B's poultry store and drove one of the fleet delivery trucks—five-window Chevrolet manual-shift pickups. My dad was the main man in charge of maintaining the fleet at night. He always worked over and beyond the normal workday to provide for his family.

One night after dinner, my dad said, "Skippy, let's go out to the alley and work on the truck." In those days, alleys were paved service drives used for the trash pickup and as a way of entering the garages. Our garages faced the alleys and were located behind the houses. I often helped my dad repair something, and felt like his right-hand man.

When I was a child, turn signals did not come standard on vehicles and were a relatively new invention for automobiles.[4] Prior to the invention of turn signals, drivers stuck their arms out of the window to inform the driver behind them that they would be turning left. Sticking one's arm out the window in those days—that was good enough. My grandfather asked my dad to install a new technology on his fleet of delivery trucks—electric turn signals. Today they are standard equipment, even though many drivers do not use them.

Example of the turn signals Dad and I installed on the delivery trucks.

I learned a lot from watching my dad work on cars. I would sit quietly and observe as he did the necessary repairs and modifications—it was a treat for me, even though I was only four years old at the time. The turn signal units bolted onto the steering column and were shiny chrome. He showed me how they worked, and my job was to hold the lever down

---

[4] In *Who Invented the Automobile?*, Brian Williams explains that the golden age of the industry was from the 1930s to the 1950s, when the car industry grew worldwide. In the United States, drivers indicated a turn using hand signals until 1938, when powered indicators appeared on Buick cars.

to enable him to check to see if they were installed properly. I felt ten feet tall sitting behind the wheel as I listened to his commands. "OK, Skip, hold down to the left. OK, lift up the lever so I can check the right."

As they flashed, a red indicator light would come on to inform the driver the turn signals were in use. I had a great time doing this and thought I was really big stuff! These memories of my father working with his hands left a positive impression on me. Yes, I truly felt cool driving all over Detroit helping my dad deliver poultry.

Moving to Saint Clair Shores

1954

I was four years old when my parents thought it would be a good idea for me to start school early. I attended kindergarten for a short period, and all I remember about it was lying down with a blanket and taking a nap.

In 1955, my parents decided to move to Saint Clair Shores. I didn't complete kindergarten, and who knows what I missed—maybe my ABCs? During this time, my mother became "that way." (This is the expression Italians used instead of the word *pregnant*.) Soon I had another sister.

To me, Saint Clair Shores seemed like miles and miles from Detroit, and maybe it was. We moved into a home of our own with a detached one-and-a-half car garage. A few years later, this garage would be where I began my hands-on career. Our new home was approximately nine hundred square feet with a full basement. We were the first house on the corner, across from a busy three-lane road. We had a full-grown maple tree in the front of the house and my job was raking up the leaves every fall.

My older sister and I were still very close. I felt terrible the day she left me to attend school two blocks away. I didn't want her to go and leave me behind, but away she went. Missing her, I walked into the school to look for her. I saw her sitting at her desk in the classroom. I knocked on his classroom door, saw her teacher, Mr. Gizoni, and told him "My mom wants my sister to come home." Needless to say, he would not let her leave, and my sister said to me, "Frankie, you have to go back home now." Just think how times have changed.

First Grade at Wheat Elementary

1955

Soon it was my turn to begin school. My parents enrolled me in first grade in the fall of 1955. I was only five years old and a big guy for my age. Although I looked six, I was not really ready to begin school at five. School was difficult for me; I needed the lessons repeated a few times. I didn't know why. I was a slow learner, so I stayed out of the teacher's view as long as I could. I kept to myself and laid low, and didn't raise my hand to ask questions.

As the teacher moved about the classroom, I never made eye contact for fear I would be called on to respond. My test scores were not the best, and I struggled with school. It wasn't easy for me. One day, when I entered my classroom, I saw that our seats were rearranged. I wondered why. In those days, the schools categorized everyone based on his or her performance. There were three groups of students: the A group, who were the bright and high achievers, the B group, who were the middle-of-the-road students, and the C group, who were those students with low academic performance. I was a C.

Educators can make or break a child's future development. I didn't enjoy attending school, especially in the C group. C-group children felt that they were different and looked down at. The brightest students got the attention, and we were often overlooked and ignored, as long as we didn't misbehave. I understood this structure, and later realized that being placed in the C group turned out to be useful to me.

Parochial School

1958

During the fall of 1958, my older sister and I were sent off to Catholic school, where I began the fourth grade at the age of eight. The school was relatively new and about ten blocks from our home. Our teachers were Dominican nuns who knew how to use yardsticks and rulers. These weren't used to teach us to measure, but to teach us to give the correct answers and not misbehave. If you didn't learn, you were belittled or smacked around a few times. Fear was the motivational factor for learning.

We wore uniforms proudly: pink shirts and brown slacks. This was a brand-new environment for me. I said to myself, "No more A, B, or C groups—hurrah!"

Or so I thought. But it was business as usual. There were no accommodations for students like me who had difficulty reading and understanding the lesson in textbooks or lectures. If you did not understand the lesson as the nuns taught it, the remedy was simple: multiple assignments to do at home. I loved every minute…right. And, if the homework wasn't completed, that meant, in the teachers eyes, that we were being insubordinate.

This is how the scenario usually went: the teacher made a call or sent the student home with a note. The parent (probably the father) conferenced with the teacher, and after returning home, the student (me) was given the proverbial tune-up with the razor strap. Results were guaranteed 100 percent effective: No more missing assignments!

I attended parochial school until I graduated from the eighth grade in the spring of 1963. For me, that was a great year! Chevrolet came out with the new Corvette Stingray split window, and the Four Seasons were at the top of the music charts. Oh, and I forgot to mention: no more brown and pink uniforms. Hooray!

Detroit News **Paper Route**

I was a big boy for my age and looked older that I was. The boy I hung around with then told me that his brother had to sell his paper route immediately. In those days, you had to be twelve years of age to own a paper route. Although I was only ten, I looked like I was twelve. My friend's brother contacted me and asked me if I wanted to buy his paper route. He went on to explain to me what his brother had done—breaking into the substation. I couldn't believe he would do such a thing. We just didn't do those types of things, especially breaking and entering, also known as a B&E. I went home to ask my mom and dad if I could buy his paper route, and they said yes. I paid him ten dollars, which included the route and all of his customers.

The route was on the next block over, on Yale Street in good old Saint Clair Shores. I was anxious to begin my new job as a *Detroit News* delivery boy. I learned the dos and don'ts of how to deliver the papers and manage a small business. I would ride my heavy-duty twenty-six-inch Schwinn Wasp with a springer front end to the substation. The substation was approximately one mile south of my house. I'd pick up the number of papers I needed, ride back to my route, and deliver my papers. I learned quickly from the customers: "Hey, don't walk on my lawn," or "Place the paper in between the screen door and front door." I introduced myself to my customers as I delivered the papers. Most were friendly, though there were some who just grumbled as I said, "Hello, my name is Frank Antonucci, and I am your new paper boy."

On Fridays, I would go door to door and collect sixty-five cents for the weekly paper. If they only received the paper on Sunday, the cost was thirty-five cents. There were a total of seventy-eight homes on the street, which ran from Harper Avenue to Little Mack. My route consisted of sixty-four houses that were taking the newspaper from me, and I was determined to have every house on that block taking the newspaper from me.

As I said, on Friday evenings, I would collect the money, and the following Saturday, I had to pay for the papers I had received and distributed during that week. We did this at the substation where we picked up our daily supply of newspapers for our customers. I believe the boy I purchased the route from thought there was a lot of money being kept inside and therefore he decided to rob it.

Throughout the years, I met a lot of nice people on my route and we developed a great rapport. I knew this because at Christmas time, the tips were unbelievable. I canvassed very hard in an attempt to encourage those who didn't take the paper from me to subscribe. I used every sales tactic that I knew. I even gave them the paper for free for the first two weeks, and bingo—they agreed to subscribe. I reached my goal, and everyone on Yale Street was taking the *Detroit News* from Frankie.

As I said, at Christmas time, I collected at least one dollar from each one of my customers. Wow. Seventy-eight dollars in 1960 was a lot of money. I was now a rich ten-year-old! I didn't know at the time that this paper route would mold and change my life.

I couldn't put a price on this experience. The lessons I learned were responsibility, dependability, experiencing many different customer personalities, financial awareness, and, most of all, financial independence from my parents. If I wanted something that was not in the norm, I would purchase it with my own funds. Earning and paying my way was a great experience for me. Managing money is not an easy task, but it's a way of life. Parents, take note. I highly recommend that you teach your children how to manage money as soon as they know how to add and subtract. I would also recommend that your children begin working as soon as they are able to do so. Start with small responsibilities such as making their beds, emptying the trash, and helping Mom clear off the dinner dishes. Hold them accountable, and be a parent. Working and responsibility are the foundation for their future. Here I was, ten years old and becoming more and more financially independent from my parents.

As my customer base expanded, I was very proud. However, I craved my father's approval. I soon began to spread my wings, and I began a bicycle repair shop in our garage. I repaired bicycles for the kids in the neighborhood for a nominal fee. I also built wagons from scrap and rented them out for the day. I believe the fee was five cents for the entire day. My customer base was limited.

Vincent

I had an early childhood friend whom I will never forget. His name was Vincent. He lived about nine houses west of us, closer to the Little Mack side of the street. Vincent was taller and bigger than I was and had a few teeth missing. He was starting to show signs of acne. I saw him one day while I was riding my shiny red Schwinn bicycle in front of his house.

Example of my shiny red Corvette Schwinn bicycle

He looked at me, and I nodded my head as all cool guys did, acknowledging his presence, and kept on riding back to my house. A few days later, Vincent walked down to my house and saw me working on my Schwinn. I was in the process of polishing the shiny stainless-steel fenders and the bright-red candy-apple paint. I said to him as cool as I could be, "Hey," nodding my head.

He didn't return the salutation or say anything back to me. I asked him, "What's your name?"

He tried to speak, but it was a language I wasn't familiar with and had never experienced. Vincent couldn't pronounce his words or speak very clearly. I knew something was different about him but didn't know what that was. I attempted to talk with him verbally for a few minutes without any success. I showed him my Schwinn and continued polishing my prized possession. Vincent looked on with enthusiasm as if he wanted to talk with me. Deep down inside, I felt sorry for him. I thought he must have been born this way, and I didn't understand what his problem was or how to fix it. Then mom called me in for dinner: "Frankie! Time for you to come in and set the table for dinner. Your father is on his way home."

It was time for me to finish up, put everything away and say good-bye to my new friend Vincent. A few days later, I went down to Vincent's house and talked to his older sisters, Lois and Laura. I wanted to find out more about Vincent and why I couldn't understand him. They thanked me for befriending him and then told me he was mentally retarded. I felt sorry for him and tried to help him talk; I really didn't understand why he was like this.

I was nine or ten years old at the time. During the sixties, being referred to as retarded was normal, and feeling sorry for someone like Vincent was acceptable. Today we think differently; it would be inappropriate to feel sorry for people with disabilities or special needs and disrespectful to refer to them as *retarded*. I could minimally understand Vincent.

21

Eventually, we learned to communicate with each other and our friendship grew. I wasn't aware of Vincent having anybody to hang out with his own age. He might have, and I didn't know.

Sometimes, I tried to make him laugh. However, because his face was slightly distorted from his birth defect, I couldn't determine whether he was laughing or not. All I knew was that here was a person around my age whom I wanted to try to help not be the way he was. I didn't realize he could never be like me, but I sure tried to help him overcome his disabilities. Being all alone is tough; not having any friends to hang out with is even tougher.

Vincent and I had some great times together. We saw each other whenever I wasn't busy doing chores around the house or delivering my newspapers. As time passed, I began to understand him more often and he understood me, and it seemed that there wasn't any difference in our verbal communication at all. I taught Vincent how to ride a bicycle, using my prized possession—my cool red butterfly-handlebar Schwinn. (I was Mr. Cool because in those days, if you owned a Schwinn, you were very cool.)

My dad was very talented and decided to build me a go-kart powered by a gasoline Briggs and Stratton engine. Wow, can you imagine how cool that was going to be? I could hardly wait for it to be finished. Dad and I went to the store to buy the steel and began to design the body and frame. He made it out of square tubing and welded it all together. It had a foot brake for stopping, a real gas pedal for acceleration and a cool little steering wheel. The front wheels were large soap box derby wheels and the rear wheels were small and wide, just right for burning rubber. We painted it using a homemade air compressor my dad made; the color was bright-red Rust-Oleum.

That kart was the envy of all who saw it, especially all the kids on my street, so I was cool too. Vincent came down to see me and my shiny red new go-kart. The kart was made for one person, and didn't have room for any passengers.

Example of a 1960's period go-kart

Vincent would watch me drive my go-kart down the street and I knew he wanted to drive it also.

I wanted Vincent to enjoy the same experiences I had and believed I could teach him how to drive it safely. There were no helmets or safety equipment in the 1960s. I didn't give it much thought about the consequences if something happened. All I wanted to do was teach my buddy Vincent how to drive my new shiny new red go-kart so he could have a lot of fun.

I carefully explained to Vincent how to sit down in the seat—he barely fit into it—then I showed him and explained how the pedals worked. "Vincent," I said, "the pedal on the right is the brake. The pedal on the left is the gas...understand me?"

Vincent nodded his head yes. I walked behind the kart and pulled the cord to start the Briggs and Stratton. On the third pull, the motor fired up, and Vincent was about to prepare for the time of his life—driving my go-kart. I watched him drive down Erben with my fingers crossed that he would be safe and not run into anything. Vincent was doing great until, as he was turning around to head back to my house, the unthinkable happened. He cut the wheel too close to the curb, lost control of the kart and hit the curb. I heard the welded wheel being torn off from its mounting bracket. At first, I was mad, but I quickly got over it because I was now in the hot seat.

I thanked God that Vincent was not hurt. He didn't show any signs of being frightened by the accident. I knew I had to do something quick before my dad found out. He wouldn't have understood why I had let Vincent drive the kart. This would have appeared to be irresponsible, even if I was just trying to give my special friend a new and exciting experience.

We brought the kart home to our garage, and Vincent and I removed the broken piece. I took it over to Manny's Sinclair gas station and asked Manny if he would weld the bracket back in place.

He said, "I will get right on it." After the part cooled off from the weld, I brought it back home and reinstalled the front wheel. I used some red touch-up paint to cover any signs of my go-kart's crash. I never said anything to anyone. I was afraid I would be in big trouble with my dad.

As time passed, Vincent and I grew closer to our teen years and we didn't see each other like we used to. In those days, people with his condition were usually institutionalized.

Vincent didn't have a father that I knew of, or at least I never saw him, and I knew his mom worked during the day. In the sixties, it was unusual for the mother to be working outside of the home. His mom told me that Vincent was getting more difficult to take care of and was having violent outbursts at home with his two sisters. She explained to me that Vincent had to be institutionalized, and he asked about me all the time and wanted to see me. I did not see or attempt to see Vincent again before he left.

I have asked myself many times why I didn't take time out to see him, and I regret it to this day. One day in the early sixties, Vincent's mom came down and told me Vincent had passed. I didn't know what to say. I felt this huge golf ball in my throat and choked up. I have never forgotten Vincent. As I moved on in my life, many of my family and students benefited from my life's lesson from Vincent. I promised I would never fail them or let them down.

Rest in peace, Vincent Hoffer.

My passion for cars

I have always had a passion for cars as long as I can remember. I enjoyed looking at them, polishing, critiquing and dreaming about the car I would one day drive. When I saw a car that was smashed from an accident or being towed to the body shop for repairs, I had an adrenaline rush inside me. I didn't know why or how the damage happened. I asked my dad more than once if we could buy a car that was wrecked and fix it. He'd say, "Yeah, that would be nice," just to pacify me.

I loved to work with my hands and build or repair things, especially vehicles. As I delivered my daily papers, I passed and critiqued the many different makes and models my customers owned. I'd see a super clean 1956 two-door hardtop lime-green-and-black Chevrolet Bel Air that was spotless and well maintained. Under the hood was a 265 V-8 with the power pack option—very cool. And a few houses farther down the street was a 1953 Pontiac that had seen better days and was ready to be traded in. There was one particular house on my route I looked forward to delivering the paper to. This guy always had the coolest cars on the block—not just one, but three or four.

It was obvious he was car collector and had the coolest cars around: a 1932 Ford rumble seat with faded original black paint and tan mohair interior; a 1932 Ford Vicky, dark blue with gray fenders, slightly customized in its day; a 1958 Chevrolet Impala convertible in a medium-blue metallic color, powered with a tri-power 348; and a bright-red 1962 two-door Dodge Coronet 440. When he started the engine in that Dodge, the ground shook.

I'd see this guy talking to his buddies around his cars and wondered who he was. In those days, you did not interrupt someone, especially an adult. You waited for the right moment to introduce yourself. He always had someone around him, so I had to wait. One day he walked up to me as I handed him the newspaper, and the timing was right. I said, "My name is Frank, and I like all the cool cars you always have around here."

He said, "Nice to meet you, Frank. My name is also Frank." Wow here I was, ten years old, meeting and talking to my favorite car guru. I didn't want to seem too inquisitive, but he saw the glow in my eyes and we connected with each other. I wanted to be cool, so I simply said, "Take it easy. I have to finish my route." I got back on my red Schwinn and pedaled off to the next house.

I couldn't wait for the next day to deliver the paper to Frank's house again. He lived with his parents, and he had a sister and a younger brother. His brother was three years older than me, and Frank was about ten years older. I didn't see him again until a few weeks later. He was waiting outside on the sidewalk for me. He said, "Frank, when you are finished with your route, stop by. I want to show you something in my garage."

Oh my God! I was so excited. Was I now a part of his in-crowd? I wondered what he wanted to show me. In the sixties, we didn't worry about all of the crazy stuff we read and hear about today. I felt safe, and after all, it was broad daylight.

I parked my red Schwinn carefully in his driveway, out of the way and using the kickstand as I didn't want to have it fall and get scratched. After all, this bike was my pride and joy. Frank opened the huge door of his two-car garage, and much to my surprise, I saw a black-and-red 1956 Ford Fairlane Crown Victoria sitting on jack stands. (Jack stands were used to support and secure a car from falling and doing great bodily harm to the person who was working on the car.) I saw a small electric drill with a grinding disc on it lying on the floor next to the left front fender.

Frank asked, "Do you know how to use fiberglass?"

I said, "No."

"Want to learn?"

I thought I had died and gone to heaven right on the spot! I said yes without hesitation. "What do you want me to do?"

He said, "We are going to repair the rust around the turn signal. First we have to grind the metal clean before we can apply the fiberglass."

"Frank," I said, "I've never done this before."

He said, "Don't worry. I will teach you." I didn't know until years later that Frank didn't know how to do this either. We were experimenting and learning together.

1956 Ford Fairlane Victoria

During the sixties, all of the cars produced had areas that were prone to rusting out, especially in a northern state like Michigan. Rock salt was and is still used on the roads to melt the ice and snow and salt will rust out the best of any vehicle. It is corrosive and causes irreparable damage and severe pitting to the chrome. Rock salt took its toll in these places on cars: 1956 Ford rocker panels and front fenders around the turn signals, 1955 Chevrolet front fenders and the infamous rear quarter panel, commonly known as the magic circles. It happened in Chrysler products, too: rocker panel and front fender caps.

Example of Frank's 1956 Ford
https://www.flickr.com/photos/42220226@N07/22571147713[CC BY-SA 2.0
*(*https://creativecommons.org/licenses/by-sa/2.0)]

After Frank and I ground out the rusted areas on the left front fender, it was ready for the fiberglass. Frank explained to me how to mix the semi-clear sticky polyester resin. I cautiously poured just enough resin into a cup. Next, I added a few drops of clear catalyst hardener, which looked almost like water. I mixed it carefully and thoroughly with a paint stick. Frank handed me a small piece of a white cloth-like material, and told me to brush the resin onto the cloth and lay it across the gaping rust hole. Several more layers of fiberglass cloth were needed to fill the hole.

The time really flew by. I was having fun and learning at the same time. When we were done, we cleaned up the garage. It was getting late and I had to get home for dinner. I couldn't wait until the next day to get back and see the repair I had done on that fender.

Fiberglass took up to twenty-four hours to cure. I picked my newspapers up earlier than usual and delivered them at a rapid pace. I kept thinking, "Why do I want to deliver papers, when all I really want to do is repair cars?" That day in

Frank's garage sparked the beginning of my long and beloved interest in auto-body repair.

My route finished, I knocked on the door and said, "Is Frank home?"

"Frankie!" his mother said. "The newspaper boy is here to see you."

He came out and said "Hi, Frank. Ready to finish the front fender?"

I waited with anticipation as I heard the springs of the garage door squeak and the door began to open. There it was—that beautiful black fender that had previously had a big rust hole through it. The fiberglass was cured and ready to be shaped with a sander. I carefully smoothed out the high spots to shape the fiberglass to follow the contour of the fender.

Then Frank said, "Ever use Bondo?"

I said, "What?"

"Bondo."

"What is it?"

"It's a filler to fill in the low spots."

Soon after that, I was mixing and spreading Bondo. When it dried, I sanded it down to prepare the fender for spray-can primer. The fender was black, so it was easy to match the color. I learned some cool stuff that week in Frank's garage—thank you, Frank.

Before long, I began to repair a few of my customers' cars on my paper route. I fixed a 1956 Chevrolet two-door Bel Air which was rusting through the fender right above the headlamps—a favorite place for the salt to viciously attack. Next was a 1954 four-door Pontiac Chieftain with the gaping holes in the right and left lower quarter panels. This is what I was born to do!

I still worked on my paper route and carried my papers in the saddlebags that the *Detroit News* provided all of its carriers. These bags fit nicely on the Schwinn carrier rack mounted securely behind my seat. I also had an auxiliary bag that mounted to the butterfly handlebars. This bag was primarily used for delivering the Sunday papers, which included all of the advertising supplements. During the week, I used this bag for my electric drill and supplies I needed for the cars I was repairing. I was on top of the world and not yet thirteen—making money with my paper route, owning a battery-operated transistor radio, learning to do auto body repair and listening to rock and roll. I was coming of age.

Our backyard garage on Erben Street proved to be more than just a one-and-a-half-car garage. It was my life! That garage rarely saw a car parked inside.

This is where it all began in our family garage on Erben

My dad had it filled with tools, a workbench, and a vice. He was a collector of anything and everything: tables and chairs, more tools, my go-kart, my wagons and my bicycles. Whatever he picked up, he made space for in the garage. He

31

saw it; he brought it home. Michigan winters can be vicious and cold, so he installed a wood-burning stove.

Now that I'd learned how to repair damaged sheet metal, I wanted to repair the rust on our family's black two-door hardtop 1957 Ford Fairlane 500. This car was cool: a two-door hardtop with a 312 cubic-inch four-barrel V-8. The Michigan salt had attacked it, and it was in badly in need of my help. The tops of the fenders above the headlamps were rusting through, and the holes in the lower rocker panels were getting larger. My dad was thinking about trading it in for a new car but the rust holes would affect the trade-in value. I didn't want to see him pay more for his new car than he had to—so, Frank to the rescue!

I asked my dad, "Can I repair the rust holes on your Fairlane?"

He was very easygoing, and much to my surprise, he agreed. I had all the tools that I needed to do the job: electric drill, sanding discs, Bondo and a lot of ambition. My dad had made a compressor that we'd used to paint my go-kart bright red. After I completed all of the rust repairs on the Fairlane body, I asked my dad to take it in for the trade-in appraisal while it was dirty. The reason for doing this was because dirt camouflaged my unprofessional bodywork. My suggestion worked. My dad received a fair trade-in value and made the deal on his new car.

Dad asked me if I wanted to go along with him to the dealer and see what he had picked out. I was dismayed to see that he had picked out a 1962 metallic-blue Ford Galaxy with a six-cylinder under the hood and an automatic transmission. Oh my God, what would all the cool guys in the neighborhood think? They'd laugh and say, "Your old man bought a six-cylinder four door!"

What could I say? I knew it was time for a makeover.

Customizing My Dad's New Ford

Back in the day, if you were seen driving or riding around in a four-door, it was not cool. My dad gave me lots of room to use my creativity and trusted the decisions and recommendations I made about doing a makeover on our new family car. If we had to ride in a four-door, I wanted it to look special and cool—in other words, bad to the bone. I was only thirteen years old, but I had read many issues of *Car Craft*, *Hot Rod*, and *Rod and Custom*. I knew about the current trends and ideas that were generated from the California custom-car scene. The first thing was to lose the small dog-dish-style factory hubcaps and stock painted-steel wheels. Dad purchased a new set of chrome reverse wheels, along with a set of four perfect baby-moon hubcaps. The tire trend was to install a set of two-inch-wide white Porta- walls, which was a less expensive way of converting a black wall tire to a whitewall.

I'd attended many car shows with my dad, and I noticed the custom cool cars were all shaved. *Shaving* in the custom-car world means removing all identifying emblems, nameplates, and logos installed on the assembly line. Shaving the hood, rear deck lid, and the right and left front fenders came easily for me. I knew this would be a priority and a must-do for a custom car. I filled the holes with liquid solder and prepped the body panels for paint. I was not equipped and experienced enough to paint these parts. They had to be color matched and look equal to (or better than) the factory paint. My dad agreed and liked the other changes I was doing to our family car. He made an appointment with the local Ford dealer and had the parts painted to match.

Example of our A 1962 Ford Galaxie

Now it was time to add a little bit of character to our car, something that no one else had on his car, maybe even something that had not even been invented yet. The car had a stainless body side molding that ran from the front edge of the front fender to the end of the rear quarter panel. This molding was approximately one and one-eighth inches wide and recessed in the center. It looked OK, but I knew I could I could make it stand out and highlight the bright metallic-blue finish even brighter. I went to the local hardware store and purchased four rolls of three-quarter-inch medium-dark blue vinyl tape. I placed the tape in the center of that shiny stainless molding just to see what it would look like. I stood back and took a look. Bingo. The color combination was spot on, and it looked great. I went into the house and asked my dad to come out and take a look. I still remember the smile on his face. He said, "Nice job. It looks great."

The makeover of our family car was complete. Now it was time to show off and get the reactions from all who saw my notable modifications.

My dad and I received many nice compliments. I needed to hear these positive reviews: *Wow! Cool!* and *Who thought of these ideas?* It felt good to listen to the affirmation. And now, when we rode to the store, I sat in the front seat.

Experiencing Grown-Up's Words

My first real-life experiences began when I took on my paper route at ten. While I picked up my newspapers at the station, I heard words I had never heard before: F—k this S—t. I thought I'd heard it all. I couldn't tell any of this to my parents because we just didn't share these types of things. My parents tried to keep us in a protected shell. However, the more we kids grew up and lived in the adult mainstream of life, the more we learned, some good and some bad. I'd hear my mom say to her friends, "So and so is in *that way*."

I asked my mom, "What does 'that way' mean?"

She replied, "Shut up, before I tell your father."

Later on I found out it meant that a woman was pregnant. This seemed very secretive and evasive— and prevented me from talking to my dad as most fathers and sons do. We blocked out dialog when it came to private matters. Another famous quote in our family was "You didn't tell anybody, did you?" They were very secretive about everything. When my dad bought his new Ford, he said, "Don't tell anybody this is our car."

I said, "Why?"

He looked me in the eye and said, "Did you tell anybody?"

In fear, I said no, but in reality, I had told a couple of buddies of mine. After all, what was I supposed to say when everyone saw a brand-new blue Galaxy in our driveway? We were very secretive and very discreet, and I never knew why.

Growing up in an Italian household was a great experience, because we had many good cultural traditions. However, when it was my turn to parent, my wife and I raised our children differently. We taught them to be open and honest with us and not to be ashamed or embarrassed to speak to us about anything. We used the word *pregnant* instead of "that way." Purchasing a new car was not a secret. However, we never wanted to brag or be boastful. My wife took care of discipline before I came home from work. Only if necessary would I address an issue with my child who might have needed a tune-up.

How about this classic statement? "Wait until your father comes home!" My mother told us this often. When we stepped out of line with my mom, we paid for our actions when our dad came home. Remember, he was a barber? His razor strap was a staple in our home and I don't recall that he ever used it to sharpen his straight razor. We were in the sixties and Schick had invented electric shavers.

Ottawa Junior High

Fall, 1963

Our Catholic school only went through the 8th grade, so I started my first year of public school when I was thirteen years old, a teenager who was beginning to discover the world.

Now that I was in junior high, the ninth grade, at a school without uniforms, I wanted to be *cool* and part of the in-crowd. Wow! What a culture shock. I couldn't believe all the fun activities and the variety of classes that were available.

I was not a sports-minded or physical type of person. My dad wanted me to play football and baseball, but these types of activities didn't interest me. If it didn't have a set of wheels, I wasn't interested in it. Oh, I would sometimes meet my friends over at the elementary schoolyard, and we played baseball. I didn't tell anyone that I was afraid of the ball and wasn't very coordinated. Watching my buddies catching, hitting, and throwing the ball and getting someone out at first base made me feel inferior. I wanted to be just like them, but sports weren't in my makeup. I could mask my inadequacies because of my size. I was good at putting on a false façade and not showing I couldn't really throw a ball.

One of the requirements of every junior high-school student was that we must have one year of physical education. Then I wished I were back in parochial school where we didn't have a gym or a class named "physical education." On my first day of gym, we met our male teacher. He wore a form-fitting T-shirt, gym shorts and white tennis shoes, and he had a chrome whistle hanging around his neck. The coach (as he wanted us to call him) gave us a list of items. He said, "Men, you need the following items to participate in my class. Write them down in your notebooks: one, a combination padlock; two, a clean bath towel; three, soap and soap tray; four, tennis shoes and white socks; five, gym shorts and a clean, not-ripped T-shirt, and six, a jockstrap."

"What the hell is going on here?" I said to myself. "Why will I need these things to run around the gym? What the hell is a jockstrap?" I had never heard of it. Man, oh man, I was more worried about being in gym than being in my English and math classes.

I talked to my dad in private and asked him, "What is a jockstrap?" I was so embarrassed to ask him but I had to know for gym class.

He briefly explained, "A jockstrap will protect your agates."

"Oh," I said. "I get it. No need to explain any further."

Well, day one was over, and I only had 179 more days to go in gym class that year.

The next day, I went down to the gym, and the coach made sure we all had the necessary items. I sat in my seat and waited patiently for him to check everyone's stuff. Then we went into the locker rooms and changed into our T-shirts and shorts. This was a new experience for me and I was very uncomfortable. Everyone was butt naked and having a good time. Oh my God, what was I doing in a locker room full of butt-naked, laughing guys?

We assembled on the gym floor, the coach gave us directions and showed us what to do: jumping jacks, push-ups, and sit-ups. Last, we ran four laps around the outside walls of the gym. The coach blew the whistle and said, "Hit the showers, and make it quick." Who in his right mind would want to take a shower with a group of guys he had never seen or talked to before? NOT ME!

That day will live in my mind forever. I was thirteen years old and just growing into manhood. Most of these kids had attended public schools from day one and they all knew each other.

One day at the end of gym class, while we were waiting to be dismissed, a cool dude named Faro pulled out of his wallet what appeared to be a foil-wrapped hand wipe and said, "Do you have one of these?"

I said, "What is it?"

He said, "It's a Trojan. Do you have one of these?"

I said, "No."

He said, "I will get you one. You'll never know when you will need it."

I said, "I am all set with that." I quickly figured out what it was, but didn't want to let on that if my mom or dad found that in my wallet, they would KILL me. Something else we didn't use in my old school.

I was a typical student who wanted to fit in and be accepted. You could smell promiscuity in the air. Coming from a strict Roman Catholic Italian family didn't exactly prepare me for this. Mom and Dad rarely addressed the everyday, common facts of life, issues, events, styles, and things we should have known as we were becoming young adults. I didn't ever question them, but I learned to communicate with my own children as they were growing into adulthood.

John F. Kennedy

November, 1963

I will never forget the day I was in Mr. Stilwell's drafting class, working on my assignment, when he walked out of the classroom and returned with tears in his eyes. He said, "Class, the president of the United States has been assassinated." It was November 22, 1963, 2:30 p.m., Dallas, Texas.

We were in shock and couldn't believe what he had said. Some started to weep. Others, like me, were mad as hell. Who would want to kill our President John F. Kennedy, and why? School was dismissed at the regular time, and as we walked across the fields, some were quiet while others were crying. This horrible tragedy was burned into our memories for our entire lifetime. I'll always remember that dark day in November—so sad.

Developing My Identity

I loved listening to all the cool rock and roll music on my eight-transistor, battery-operated handheld radio. Motown was on every station. I listened to AM 800 CKLW with the coolest of cool disc jockeys, Robin Seymour. AM Keener 13 was also cranking out the tunes. In the evening, we couldn't wait until 6:00 p.m. Then we switched the dial to AM 1270 WXYZ, and we listened to Joel Sebastian and Lee Allan with his infamous horn.

The Fonz
By ABC Television (eBay item
photo front photo back)
[Public domain]

The dress code in the parochial school required all of the boys to wear a pink shirt and brown dress pants. We were not allowed to express our individual identities. During my first year of public school, I learned many new ways of being cool. I first noticed the types and styles of clothes we wore to school. The boys wore tight above-the-ankle blue jeans, white T-shirts, white socks, and a pair of black pointy-toe shoes.

40

The in-place to buy your shoes was a store named Jack's Fifth Avenue, located on the corner of Seven Mile and Gratiot in Detroit. Before we went into the store, we would drool over all of the pointed shoes he had on display in the window. The coolest of the cool had to be the most pointed shoes he had in the store. The next day at school, we'd strut down the hallway, acting cool so our peers would notice our shoes. A feature of our new shoes was the clacking sound coming from the Cuban heels—a sound that only a Cuban heel could make. People knew you were coming down the hall, and it was even cooler if you walked as if you didn't notice that sound—even if deep down inside, you were saying to yourself, "Hey people, look at me! I am Mr. Cool."

We didn't have our driver's licenses in the ninth grade. However, some of us hung around with or knew guys who had their licenses and a cool car. The girls also had their own identities and coolness about themselves: short skirts and tight blouses, pushing the boys' testosterone to an all-time high. Their hair was ratted a mile high and secured in place with hair spray. There could be ninety mile-per-hour winds, and their hair wouldn't move an inch.

There were two types of groups in school, cool kids (greasers) and frats. If you wanted to fit in and be cool, you followed the dress code of the cool kids. I never knew what peer pressure was or the meaning of it until I entered the ninth grade. Then I became a greaser.[5] A greaser was cool.

---

[5] The greasers were a working-class subculture formed by young people. It originated in the 1950s and peaked in the 1960s. This group was formed in the northern and southern United States. They were a symbol of rebellion. The subculture's name—*greaser*—came from their "greased" hairstyles. They combed back their hair using wax, creams, or gel.

Greasers
Venice Senior High School (Los Angeles) 1974 yearbook The Gondolier

In the late 1970s, there was a television program that epitomized the lifestyle of the greasers. The most popular was a program named *Happy Days*, starring (who else) Henry Winkler as the Fonz. Like those stars, our dress style was simple: tight jeans, white T-shirts, pointed shoes, greasy hair slicked back with the ever-popular Brylcreem. Or maybe a waterfall hairstyle like the popular New Yorker–style cut. Oh, I can't neglect mentioning that you had to carry a hairbrush in your back pocket on the right side, and we all had that certain strut as we walked down the hallways. I had made the transition from wearing a pink-and-brown uniform to being a cool greaser. I was now the cool one, and I didn't want to ruin my image.

The other group in our school was the *frats*[6] who dressed a bit more conservatively in madras shirts, khaki pants, and sweaters. They wore their hair long but not all greased up. The boys and girls who dressed in this style resembled Dustin Hoffman and Katharine Ross in *The Graduate*.

---

[6] A *frat* (from *fraternity*) was a youth who dressed neatly and conformed to the accepted conservative styles.

Lakeview High School

Fall, 1964

I began my first year of high school in the tenth grade. My high school was called Lakeview High, home of the Huskies. It was located on Eleven Mile Road in Saint Clair Shores. As I walked through the main front doors on my first day, I couldn't believe how big it was. Wow! I began to see many of my old friends from the parochial school I had attended.

The changes and culture of being in a new environment were again overwhelming in the beginning. The classrooms were numbered, and there was a second floor in this school. I needed to become familiar with my surroundings because when the bell rang, everyone had to be in his or her assigned seat. If you were caught in the hallways after the second bell rang, you were sent to the principal's office and received the "wood." Now, we all know what the wood is, don't we? *Wood* was another term for the paddle, but the word *wood* seemed more grown-up. I was never sent down to the office for the wood, although a couple of my buddies received it, and when they came out of the principal's office, they had tearing eyes.

We had other things happen that year. In February of 1964, we were invaded by the Beatles. The war in Vietnam continued to escalate. My priority was to finish school.

Algebra Class

My desire to be cool was at an all-time high, so I will never forget my most embarrassing day in class in high school. In elementary school, I was placed in the C group and that stigma of not measuring up to the other kids in my class stayed with me all the way through school. I never forgot being looked down upon. I felt different from the others. I would never be as smart as they were. (Much later I realized the adverse effects of being labeled helped me become an effective and positive teacher, but that was still far away in my future.) Math class wasn't my strongest subject, and it was a required course. I needed to take it to graduate from high school. I thought this time things would be better, with a new school, new environment and new teachers.

I walked into the classroom and noticed the bulletin boards were covered with posters from around the world. The desks were perfectly aligned. I wanted to sit in the back row. Sitting there would allow me to maintain a low profile, stay out of the teacher's sight. As I knew, math wasn't my best subject, and that semester could be a long and drawn-out affair. Therefore, I had to suck it up and quickly find my seat.

As I walked across the room, I was cool and confident. After all, no one knew I had been in the C group during my elementary years. Unfortunately all the seats in the back of the classroom were taken, and the only seat I saw available was in the front row. Sitting there made it too easy for me to look out the window and daydream.

I listened attentively as the teacher introduced herself. "Hello, my name is Ms. Kowalchak, and I will be your algebra teacher for this semester." She stood about five foot four. She had dyed-blond hair and wore heavy makeup to cover the scar she had around her right eye. I wondered about that scar. How did she get it? Did she have an eye transplant? As she strutted around the classroom, the aroma of her Chanel No. 5 was strong. As she taught us the lesson, she'd periodically walk up to the chalkboard to write down an equation for clarification purposes. She wrote something like this: $A + 2 \, sq. = p. \, to \, left \, degree\ldots$

I was totally lost and confused, and I didn't understand any of it. I began to sweat and realized if I didn't understand it from the beginning, I would be lost forever and fail the class. My heart started to pound and I felt the blood rushing through my veins. I wanted to raise my hand and ask a question, but I felt intimidated by her demeanor. I prayed she wouldn't call on me to answer any questions. "Please, God. I will not have any more impure thoughts. Please don't have her ask me any questions. I promise I will be good." I stayed quiet . . .

In five minutes the dismissal bell would ring, and she asked the class the classic question, "Do you have any questions for me?"

I'd heard that many times and was always afraid to raise my hand. I thought, "What the heck. I'll be truthful." So I raised my hand and said, "I do not understand how to do algebra equations."

She said to me (and I quote), "You're too stupid to understand the lesson."

The whole class burst out laughing as if I were giving the teacher a hard time. I was totally embarrassed, to say the least. If I could disappear through the cracks in the tiled floor, this would have been the time to do so.

The dismissal bell rang, and as I was getting ready to exit her class, I wanted to say to her, "Good-bye, Ms. Scarface. I am not coming back to your class." I knew if I said that, I would have an automatic free pass to the principal's office and receive the wood. My dad would receive a phone call from the main office, and I would get a razor strap across my backside when he came home from work. I chose to keep my mouth closed and not say a word.

I walked out her classroom in true greaser form, walked straight down to my counselor and dropped the class. I never enrolled in another algebra class again.

That moment would become a pivotal point in my life. How many times have kids had this happen to them or a loved one? We are all entitled to receive encouragement, to be understood and not be talked down to. Those who become successful reach their goals through encouraging words and support, not discouraging words. Some of us never receive the positive reinforcement we so often crave.

I didn't get the encouragement I craved as a youngster, yet, later found and used my God-given talents to excel in areas that I was really good at. Those talents earned me approval and positive strokes. I wish everyone would think about the words they say before they say them. Words we choose to say can leave emotional scars in someone forever.

Our Family Had Grown

By the year 1963, I had four sisters and two brothers. My mom was a stay-at-home mom because that was how it was for the American family during the 1950s through the '70s. Dad worked, while Mom raised the children and managed the daily duties of running the house. We owned one car, one television, and one phone.

In the 1960s, to use a phone we dialed a phone number in a circular motion and waited for an automated system or human operator at a switchboard to connect our call with the receiving person. In our house, we had the basic phone service, which was a party line.[7] And, oh, did we have fun with the party line. There were times my sister and I would pick up the phone and listen in on the party line. We would put our hands over our mouths so the person talking on the phone couldn't hear us breathing and laughing. We thought this was so funny.

We did this, of course, only when our parents were not home because we were told it was illegal to listen in. Once in a while, the talkers would hear our voices or laughter, and we were abruptly warned, "Hang up the phone! I am going to call the police on you kids right now." We were scared shitless, thinking that if the cops showed up at our house, we would be going straight to jail. We also knew we would be disgracing the Antonucci name, and our dad would give us a tune-up with the razor strap.

As teenagers growing up in the sixties, we began to hang out with our friends as we watched programs like *American Bandstand* and *Swingin' Time*. These were thirty-minute television programs that featured singing by popular recording artists—our idols.

The audience consisted of teenagers like us dancing to the music. We saw the latest dancing trends, hairstyles, and clothes. We couldn't wait to see the person who sang our favorite songs, the ones we listened to every day on our transistor radios. *American Bandstand* was a syndicated program hosted and produced by a disc jockey out of Philadelphia, Pennsylvania, named Dick Clark. We couldn't

---

[7] A party line (multiparty line, shared service line, party wire) was a local loop telephone circuit shared by multiple telephone service subscribers. Only one party at a time could use a shared telephone line. If someone was already talking on it, you had to try later or wait to make your call.

wait to come home from school and watch *American Bandstand*. In the beginning of the show, Dick would say who his special guest was. "Today, here to sing his smash hit 'The Twist,' is our good friend Chubby Checker . . . "

We sat patiently, though excited, waiting for those infamous words to come out of Chubby's mouth. "There's a new dance and it goes like this..." You guys know the rest. One of my favorites was Dion[8]. He was a true greaser, right down to the waterfall hairstyle. When he sang "Teenager in Love," coolness was at an all-time high for me. "Each night, I ask the stars up above / Why must I be a teenager in love?"

We were impressionable teenagers who thought the sixties were great. We didn't think about current events happening around us like the realities of the Cold War, communism and the fighting going on in Vietnam. Those happened in a faraway land, and wouldn't affect us—or so we thought. My motto was, "Remember the good times, and forget the bad."

In the sixties, my dad was a barber at a new place, the Eastland Center Shopping Mall. As the years passed, my father and I weren't as close as we had been when we delivered chickens for my grandfather. Maybe it was because the family was growing or I was maturing and pulling away. I didn't know. I often felt bad for my dad and wondered how he could make enough money to support all of us, nine including Mom, all us children and himself. He worked long hours at the barber shop. (The barber shop's hours of operation were the same as the operating hours of the

---

[8] Dion Francis DiMucci (born July 18, 1939) was better known as Dion, an American **singer and songwriter** whose work has incorporated elements of doo-wop, rock and R&B styles.

shopping mall.) Many nights during the week we were in bed before he came home because we had to get up early in the morning for school. It was a special treat for us if my dad had the day off during the week—but that didn't happen very often.

I never knew how much money he made because that was another question we didn't ask our parents. He was a good provider, because we never went without or felt deprived. If we asked for something with frills on it, he would say, "That's good. Now go out and work for it."

I wanted the finer things in life but didn't want to be a burden or deprive my siblings of anything. It wouldn't be fair. So, I began to work harder and become more and more independent. I felt the gap between us widen and missed my earlier times spent with him. I also felt guilty that he had to support all of us, so I explored my options and spread my wings. I was coming into my own as Frank Antonucci.

Yet, I was obedient and the oldest Italian son. Whatever I was asked to do, I did without hesitation. I never wanted to disgrace our family name. My parents were proud people and didn't want anyone to talk about us because our family name could be tarnished and disgraced with gossip or a scandal. Now, as I reflect on that era, I say to myself, "Wow, have times changed."

I constantly craved my parent's approval and encouragement, because I seldom heard these words: *I am proud of you. You're a good son. I love you.* Who knows? Maybe they wanted to say it but couldn't. Parents' words can be pivotal in their children's' lives and a deciding factor in whether they become successful or failures.

Even though we'd once been close, and even though I'd won awards, earned college degrees and been very successful in my career, the last words my father said to me before he passed away were these: "You have been a big disappointment to me as a son."

I was crushed, to say the least. My reply was not out of anger but love for my father. I said to him, "My entire life, I wanted you to be proud of me and tell me so. I became the man I am because I wanted your approval. It doesn't matter what you say to me. I will always love you." A short time later, he passed away.

As adults, we need to be careful what we say, because our words can make or break another's soul.

D&W Standard Service

February 1963

At the ripe old age of thirteen as my interests began to change, I said good-bye to my paper route. Although I had accomplished my goal of having every household on Yale Street subscribe to the *Detroit News*, it was no longer enough for me. I wanted more. I no longer felt the gratification and challenge I had felt earlier, and my route had become routine. The profits were great, especially during my Christmas collection, but I was ready to move on and expand my knowledge of working on cars.

On the corner of Harper and Erben stood a Standard Gas station. I thought about how convenient it would be for me if I could get a job working there where I could walk to work. Even though I knew how to drive and had sneaked the car out of the driveway a few times, at thirteen I was years away from getting my driver's license. After school one day, I decided to walk across the busy three-lane road and introduce myself to the station owners. The day was clear, and the smell of greasy French fries came out of the fan of the Coney Island located right next to the station.

I walked into the office and announced, "Hi, my name is Frank Antonucci, and I wonder if you guys are looking for any help."

The two owners were sitting down. They acted as if I weren't even standing there, but finally looked at me and said, "What do you know?"

I felt the sweat running down the side of my cheek. Here I was, thirteen and asking for a job at a gas station. I was heading for the major leagues now. I responded, "Oh, I have a lot experience working with tools with my dad, and I am willing to learn." I went on to say, "I have a go-kart, and I know how to change the spark plug. Oh yeah, I also work on my Schwinn bicycle."

The interview lasted approximately ten minutes, and they put me to work immediately. I thought, "How cool will this be? Working on cars and wearing a uniform. Does it get any better than this?"

Here again, my knowledge and size and not my age worked to my advantage. This was a two-service-bay, full-service station that also sold regular and premium leaded gasoline. I saw a 1962 Impala convertible waiting to have a rebuilt 409 V-8 engine installed, and a 1962 short-bed F-150 in need of a clutch. I felt I was in car utopia.

There were two owners: Kenny Wall, who was from Houston, Texas, and Ray Dixon, from Nashville, Tennessee. What a combination. Kenny was cool and smooth and much younger than Ray. Kenny drove a burgundy four-speed 390 horsepower 1964 Galaxy 500 that was bad to the bone. Ray drove a 1963 metallic-blue Oldsmobile Delta 88 convertible. Until the mid-1970s, gas stations were designed to service automobiles. They sold gas and oil, but not milk, bread, cappuccino, and lattes. I began working with a skilled but temperamental mechanic named Larry. I thought he was too cool. He drove a white partially primed 1956 Ford T-Bird two-seater, powered by a fine-tuned 312 cubic-inch V-8 that sounded sweet. He had installed a dual glasspack exhaust system and a three-speed manual transmission. A glasspack exhaust system would make your car sound like a lion's roar and let everyone know you were coming down the street. This was a very popular exhaust system in the fifties and sixties.

Larry didn't say much, but he did a lot of whistling. Maybe he had a nervous condition. I never asked him. That first day, I wondered why he was so quiet and mild mannered.

On my second day, Larry asked me to give him an open-end five-eighths combination wrench he needed for the repair he was doing. I said OK. I went over to his big red Snap-on toolbox, which was parked next to his workbench, and I began to look for the five-eighths combination he wanted.

He said, "What the f——k is taking you so long? What the f——k? Are you making it?"

Holy shit! This guy could talk! He wasn't whistling any longer, he was pissed! I knew I had better bring him something pretty quick if I didn't want to get fired on my second day on the job. So I guessed, and wouldn't you know it, I brought Larry the mechanic the wrong size. I thought he was going to kill me right then and there. He threw the wrench across the room and began to scream, "You stupid, no-good motherf—ker. I never saw anybody as f—king stupid as you. Did you know that each of the wrenches are clearly marked with the sizes on each end?"

I said, "No."

He said, "The next time you do not know what it is I am asking you to get, just ask me. DO YOU UNDERSTAND?"

I quickly ran across the street to our home and changed my underpants. Larry taught me a lesson I never forgot. Wow, what an interesting first couple of days at my new job. At first, I thought I was going to tell my dad what Larry had said, and then I thought, "What is my dad going to do?" I never said a word to him but remembered this experience for the future. Welcome to the real world of work.

As I matured and gained more experience, Larry and I got along just fine. I was (and am) a hands-on learner, and Larry saw this talent in me. I learned by doing things with my hands. My mind absorbed all of the new information that Larry began to teach me. I learned so much that I felt like a sponge soaking up water. I was amazed I learned so quickly. The days I spent working with Larry were fun and exciting. I couldn't wait to go to work the next day and learn more.

As time passed, Larry moved on, and I turned fifteen years old. I soon became the new Larry and worked many hours after school and full-time during the summer. I will always appreciate him for the many things he taught me. We learn from our mistakes and experiences. Thank you, Larry, for teaching me to do things the right way.

My 1964 Galaxy 500

Although the gap widened between my dad and me, he still believed in me and supported my dreams to work on car bodies. I continued to work many long hours at D&W Standard, and most of the time, my work week went like this: Monday through Friday, 12:30 p.m. until closing time at 11:00 p.m. Saturdays and Sundays, 9:00 a.m. to 11:00 p.m. I worked as much as I could. I loved the job and the money. During the summers, my hours were unlimited. I wasn't going to have to scrounge around for anything in life. After all, I was Mr. Big! The money rolled in, and now I could do anything I wanted to do—within reason, that is.

Before I turned sixteen years old, I bought and sold a few cars—nothing much, just small-time lumpy rides. (A *lumpy* was a car that had seen better days and was a few steps away from the scrapyard.) One of these lumpies was a 1958 Plymouth Savoy with a straight cylinder engine and a three-speed manual transmission. I also purchased a 1960 two-door Plymouth Belvedere with a rod knock. I purchased these lumpies in the hopes of making a few dollars by flipping them for some quick, easy cash.

I didn't wait to take driver's training through the normal process at Lakeview High School. In those days, public schools offered those who were fifteen years of age free driver's training classes. I didn't want to wait that long to receive my driver's permit, so I signed up to take my driver's training class at the local YMCA. It cost $150.00 and I had the money to pay for it.

In Michigan, you could get your learner's permit at the age of fifteen. This enabled you to drive as long as there was an adult sitting in the passenger's seat. I wanted the permit to be the coolest of the cool. I would be one step closer to driving down the street with my favorite tunes blasting and the wind blowing through my thick black greased-back hair. I visualized myself driving with the Beach Boys singing: *"And she'll have fun, fun, fun 'til her daddy takes the T-Bird away..."*

Such sweetness was just around the corner and within my reach. The big day was coming: February 26, 1966. Would you believe, on that day Michigan had a record snowstorm? Everything was closed. Schools closed, stores closed, and yes, the Michigan Secretary of State closed too! Maybe this was a message from God—who knows?

We celebrated my birthday in true family tradition. My mom made...well, what else is there? Spaghetti for me, and my favorite kind of cake—cherry nut. So yummy. It was time to blow out the candles and open my present. Yes, singular "present." We didn't have *presents* because a single gift was sufficient for us. I slowly opened the thinly wrapped package, wondering what it could be. Much to my surprise, it was a brand-new set of license plates for the 1964 Ford Galaxy 500 I had purchased with my dad's help before I turned sixteen. I had paid for it, but he had to sign for it and put the title in his name. I didn't know why. I guess that was how they did it in those days.

In the days prior to all of the technology and computers, we read the daily newspaper. I read the automotive classified ads daily to see what was for sale. I saw an ad for a 1964 Ford Galaxy 500 XL. I had called the number and in a deep, adult voice said, "Hello, I am calling you about the '64 Ford you have advertised. Can you tell me about the car?"

The owner described the Galaxy as I salivated on the other end of the phone. I asked him for his address and arranged to take a look at it with my dad. Fortunately the guy lived only about four miles from us—perfect.

The big day was here. I hopped in my dad's car, and we drove to the man's house to look at the car. This car was me, all the way. I lifted the hood and saw a beefed-up, 390-cubic-inch, single four-barrel carburetor, Holman Moody heads, and a Crower cam, four-speed transmission, 411 rear end, factory headers and a dual exhaust. The color was black on black.

My dad always liked to negotiate the asking price, so I stood back and listened. I never interrupted him as he was trying to make a deal to buy the car for less than the asking price. He couldn't make the deal, and we drove away. I was disappointed. However, my dad knew what he was doing. He said, "Let's wait until tomorrow, and I will call him and try to make another deal to buy this car for you."

I once again began to feel close to my dad. I said, "Thanks, Dad, for doing this for me. I trust your decision." That night I couldn't sleep. I kept thinking about that black 1964 Galaxy 500. The next day, my dad called the guy around noon, and the guy said he had just traded it in to the local Ford dealer in East Detroit. I was crushed. I said to my dad, "Let's go to the dealer and see how much they are asking for it."

We hopped in the car and drove to the dealer. As we pulled up to the used car office, there she was—that drop-dead, bad-to-the-bone Galaxy 500. She was just sitting there, waiting for a new owner.

My dad asked the sales manager, "How much for that black Ford?"

He said, "Twenty-four hundred dollars."

My dad said, "Is that the best price you will take for it?"

The dealer said, "How much do you want to pay for it?"

Originally, the man who owned it wanted $2,200, so we offered $1,800. No go. My dad offered $2,000, and the dealer still said no.

"How about two thousand, one hundred and fifty?" the dealer said. My dad agreed. "Come on in, and we will write up the deal."

I didn't have my driver's license yet, but my dad let me drive that car home and park it in the driveway until I got my license. In those days, things were different. If I were caught driving without a license, who knows what would have happened to me? I took my chances and played it cool and got back to Erben Street without incident.

After the big snowstorm of 1966 was over and the roads were cleared and safe enough to drive on, I made an appointment with the Secretary of State and scheduled my final road test. I must admit, I almost drove myself to that office on Ten Mile Road, but I didn't want to take a chance. I was too close to driving my car legally. My mom had taken my dad to work that day so she drove me over for the road test. Within an hour of my arrival, I walked out the front door with my Michigan driver's license. I was now a legal, licensed driver! No longer would I have to keep looking into the rear-view mirror for the cops.

Or so I thought. There were days I cruised down Harper, and everyone knew I was coming. As I passed the girls, I would downshift into second gear just to hear the exhaust backing down and making that cool rattling sound. I will admit my driving skills weren't the best. I was a true-blue hot rodder.

We lived walking distance from the school, so there wasn't a need for me to drive my car. I walked every day and left the car home in the driveway. After all, I didn't want anybody to put any fingerprints on its mile-deep black-paint finish. I would tell my buddies about the car, but they had never seen it. Some might have even thought I was giving them a story or really didn't have the car that I talked so much about because they never saw it.

I finally decided it was time to show it off in front of Lakeview High School. The weather was perfect, and I was in the mood to drive my car. The sun was shining bright, and I could smell the fresh air coming from Lake Saint Clair. There was not a cloud in the sky, and the humidity was low—a perfect spring day. I ran home for lunch and ran into the house to get the keys.

My mom said, "Why are you home right now?"

"I want to take my car out for a ride."

"Be careful," she said.

"OK, bye."

I put my key into the ignition and began to crank it over. All it took was one pump of gas into that huge Holey four-barrel carburetor. Oh, the sweet sound of the headers and exhaust. I slowly put that four-speed transmission into reverse and backed out of our driveway onto Erben Street. After carefully coming to a complete stop, I shifted the transmission into first gear and began my journey to the high school.

I wanted the engine to be warmed up and loose because what I was about to do required skill and knowledge of how to drive a high-powered muscle car. I drove my black Galaxy carefully back to school, west on Eleven Mile Road where I saw all of the kids outside, having their lunches and talking in the Student commons area. As I passed the group, I downshifted into second gear just to hear the roar of my exhaust. They heard me and looked up. I saw some of my buddies waving to me. I knew I had gotten their attention, so I was about to make the Michigan left turnaround and perform for all to see.

I headed east, and I stopped right in front of the school. All the kids were watching me. I revved up the motor, and with my right foot on the gas and my left foot on the clutch pedal pressed to the floor, I kept my eye on the tachometer and revved the engine until the tach read six thousand RPM. I popped the clutch. The rear tires started to spew smoke from the spinning of the wheels, and the smell of burning rubber filled the clean fresh air. The sound of the engine told me to get ready to shift into second gear. Without hesitation, I power-shifted, and slammed that four-speed transmission into second as the car tried to go sideways from all that power. I said to myself, "Don't worry, kids. I have it under control." It was a perfect day for showing off. As the smoke from my spinning tires began to clear, all of a sudden I looked in my rearview mirror, saw the red flashing lights, and heard that unforgettable sound of sirens blaring. Oh, shit. By this age, I was too old to get the razor strap. However, I felt I had really let my dad down and broken the trust he had in me.

It got worse. The cop who stopped me was the notorious Saint Clair Shore's cop everyone tried to avoid—Officer Hannah. He stood about six foot five and weighed about 260 pounds. He was built like he was untouchable. His head was naturally bald, not shaved. He had a long nose and was built as solid as a rock. His attitude matched his physical appearance. He resembled the famous 1960s wrestler named Dick the Bruiser. Nobody messed around with either one of these guys.

I quickly went from being the coolest to a guy who was about to meet and receive a ticket from Officer Hannah. There was a rumor that Officer Hannah had given his grandmother a ticket, but we could never validate that. I was issued two tickets: one for excessive noise and the other for speeding.

This was just one of many of life's learning experiences. Because I was a juvenile, I had to appear in juvenile court before a judge who would tell me what my consequences would be.

As I entered the courtroom, I had to see a referee. I was sixteen and had received two moving violations only months after earning my driver's license. The referee was not thrilled to see me, and I think he might have thought I had starred in the movie *Blackboard Jungle*. Back in the day, many said I looked a little like Sal Mineo or Ritchie Valens.

Well, I received my punishment and the consequences for my actions. The referee said I would lose my driver's license for three months, and must attend a remedial driver-training course located in Mount Clemens. My dad was angry and disappointed with me. However, this tune-up was better than losing my license forever.

My parents said to me, "We are not driving you to Mount Clemens every week. Find your own ride." What the hell was I going to do now? Mount Clemens was approximately fifteen miles from Saint Clair Shores. I couldn't miss the court-ordered classes because I didn't want to end up in the juvenile home for troubled teenagers. I was not a troublemaker, even if I loved to drive fast in a fast car. I worked every day. I was not a problem in school. I had just done something…well, let's just say I hadn't used my God-given common sense. I was just being a rebellious teenager, and let's leave it at that.

I thought about the predicament I was in and I needed to come up with a game plan, quick. This was my brilliant solution: While my dad was at work and my mother was in the basement watching her soap operas, I'd carefully back my car out of the driveway and drive myself to the remedial court ordered program. My perfect plan as long as I didn't get caught. I drove my black Ford very cautiously to Mount Clemens and parked it around the corner, making it appear as if I had gotten a ride and walked into the class.

Our basement was a carbon copy of our grandparents. My mom cooked, washed clothes and spent many hours on the telephone and watching television in the basement. The upstairs was saved for company that came over to visit. The furniture in the living room was covered with clear plastic, the kitchen was never cooked in, and everything was perfect.

Detroit Autorama

1967

Another dreary Michigan winter arrived. Our winters can be brutally cold and sloppy. The roads were salt-covered, damp, and slippery. The overcast days were gloomy, and the daylight hours were short. I didn't like the winter season. I wasn't the outdoors type and didn't like building snowmen. I couldn't wait until spring arrived. This time of the year, there seemed to be a lull in our lives. The Christmas presents had all been opened; the Christmas tree was taken down, the bulbs, ornaments, and tree lights all neatly stored for the following year.

However, this year, 1967 was a very important time for me, more than I ever could have imagined. I didn't want to drive my pride and joy, my black Galaxy, on the salt-covered roads, fearing the salt was just waiting to viciously eat away at the pristine mammoth steel body. Rust is like a terminal disease. Once it begins to eat away the steel, it must be stopped. If it is not stopped quickly, it will be too late, and in the end, a once-beautiful rolling monster will be headed to the scrapyard and become a statistic. Just another rot bucket off the road. I kept it parked and didn't drive it for fear of the salt.

Oh, I forgot to mention that the remedial driver's training program didn't improve my driving skills. Shortly after I completed the program that had been ordered by the referee, I received a few more speeding tickets, and I lost my license again. This time it was for six months. There wasn't much I could say. All of my excuses were getting old: I didn't see the speed limit sign. My accelerator pedal was stuck. Officer, please don't give me a ticket. My dad will kill me if he finds out I was speeding. Can't you let me slide?

A year earlier, I began thinking about entering my 1964 Ford into the Detroit Autorama. This event was the biggest and most prestigious custom-car show in the eastern part of the United States. Custom cars were entered locally and also from around the country. If your car made it into the Detroit Autorama, you were the coolest of the cool. Every December, we couldn't wait to go to the Autorama. This event was held in the beginning of January in the fairly-new Cobo Hall convention center that was large enough to hold a thousand cars. Finally, we heard the advertisements on our transistor radios promoting this major car event. Listening to them made our adrenaline run at an all-time high. We didn't care about the gloomy and dark winter days any longer because we had something to get excited about: all the cool cars at the show.

My dad and I and my buddies went to Autorama many times, critiquing all of the cool cars on display. I'd say to myself, "One day I will have a cool car for everyone to see."

I'd seen all the cars and thought, "If this were mine, I would have done this or that modification." In August 1966 I decided that I wanted to build my first show car and enter it into the next January's Autorama. I submitted my application describing the modifications I was making, and sent a picture of the car as the work was in progress. Not all applicants made the cut. However, I received a letter in late October that my car has been accepted to be a part of the 1967 Detroit Autorama. "Congratulations!" the letter said. "Your 1964 Ford Galaxy has been accepted into the Detroit Autorama. Best of luck."

I was so excited that this competition would prove to me and everyone else what this C-group student could do. I was still searching for that almighty approval. I thought through the plan very carefully because I was about to dismantle my recently purchased 1964 Ford Galaxy from the front bumper to the rear and everything in the middle. There could be no mistakes. My car had to be flawless. I had to finish this massive stand-alone project. There was no turning back. I was going big time at the age of sixteen!

I needed a place to work on my car and our one-and-a-half-car garage on Erben wasn't big enough. I asked Ken and Ray if I could use the station after hours to build my show car. They immediately said yes. They gave me some guidelines I needed to follow: "Do not work on your car during company time. Do not have anyone hanging around here after hours, and be sure to leave the bay area clean for the next morning." Then they added, "We are excited for you and will help you any way that we can."

I needed lots of money in order to keep the massive project on schedule. Therefore, I asked Ken for a small loan. He said, "I will discuss this with Ray and get back to you." The next day, he said, "How much do you need?"

I said, "I'm not sure. I've never done a job like this."

Ken said, "Ray and I will pay for the entire project and all the bills you pile up, and at the end, we will come up with a plan. We are not giving you the money. We are loaning you the money. Do you understand?"

I said, "I understand, and thank you." I was very grateful they too believed in me.

When I attended all of the previous Autorama shows, I had made many mental notes about how, if I were to ever build a custom car, it would look. I'd remove of all identifying emblems and factory logos, modify the remaining factory moldings, remove the stationary right front fender-mounted antenna and replace it with a sunken and frenched power antenna in the left rear quarter panel.

A color change was also in the works. I repainted the entire car. My black beauty was now a mile-deep dark color called Marina turquoise—a Pontiac Bonneville color. All of the black was only a memory, including the door and trunk jambs. Under the hood was my high-performance 390 Ford dressed in chrome valve covers and with an air cleaner to match. I spent many long hours scraping and cleaning the undercarriage and prepping for paint.

1964 Ford Galaxie 500 XL 390 C.I. 330 H.P. four-speed—bad to the bone!

In those days, the dealer spayed a rubberized undercoating to protect the bottom of the chassis from road salt. I painfully removed all of it—what a mess! However, finally, it was ready to be painted and detailed for the judges. I mounted the Goodyear F-60 fourteen-inch tires, with a set of deep-dish chrome reverse wheels and baby-moon hubcaps. That was all it needed to give it that custom-show-car appearance. The interior was basically stock. The only modification was the sound system. I installed a bright chrome ARC 45 RPM record player that cranked out the tunes and was mounted under the dash, wired to a vibrosonic amplifier...oh, how I loved that sound.

Cobo Hall, Detroit   *Inside Autorama*

*I, Mikerussell [GFDL (http://www.gnu.org/copyleft/fdl.html), CC-
BY-SA-3.0 http://creativecommons.org/licenses/by-sa/3.0/)
By Joetregembo [CC BY-SA 4.0
(https://creativecommons.org/licenses/by-sa/4.0)]*

In late December, my custom Ford was ready for the big day to appear in the 1967 Detroit Autorama. My dad lined up a trailer for the day we were scheduled to take the car to Cobo Hall. I had previously received all the necessary paper work to get us through security and enter the rear entrance of Cobo Hall. The security man said, "Welcome. Do you guys have your paper work?" My dad handed him the forms, and my heart was beating fast. "OK…go on in and follow the signs."

As we made the turn and unloaded the car from the trailer, a team of Autorama staff judges came over to inspect my car for the final approval. I was sweating it out, but my 1964 Ford was now an official participant of the 1967 Detroit Autorama. For the next three days, my 1964 XL would be on display. My hard work and determination would be there for everyone to see and admire.

Detroit Autorama 1967 award winning 1964 Ford Galaxie 500 XL

My car was in the Late Model Conservative Custom Hardtop class. I later found out there were twenty-five cars in that class, and five trophies would be awarded. During the

trophy presentation, they announced fifth place, fourth place, and then I heard these words: "Now, third place for a late-model conservative custom hardtop goes to a 1964 Ford Galaxy XL belonging to Frank Antonucci!"

I was shocked and thrilled! My first time showing a custom car, and out of twenty-five cars in my class, I had won third place. Wow!

This was a proud moment for me and my family. The kids at school heard the news (even though there was no Facebook in those days) and were happy for me. Kenny and Ray were very proud. They wanted the car displayed in front of the station. I was glowing and proud of myself. That was a week I will never forget.

Plymouth Troubleshooting Contest

In the beginning of my last semester at Lakeview High School, I was enrolled in a class called cooperative education—also known as co-op. This class enabled me to attend school with a reduced schedule. I was still working at D&W Standard and loving every minute of it. I was making money and attending high school—not bad. In fact, it was great for me. One of my favorite classes was…can you guess? Ready? I loved auto shop. I had a cool, low-key teacher named Mr. Campbell. We rarely saw Mr. Campbell uptight or angry with anyone. Our class consisted of all male students who wanted to go into the automotive field. We all drove cool cars and had our bragging rights. My buddy Freddie had a 1961 Chevrolet two-door post with a beefed-up 283. It was a big car, but Fred had it fine-tuned. Then there was Alan with his 1957 red Plymouth Fury 318. He could never get it to burn out. My buddy Tom had a 1964 Mustang six-cylinder three-speed on the floor. When he used to slam second gear, he would bend the driver's seat. And who could ever forget Dave (The Fish) who drove a fast back Plymouth Barracuda?

Every year, the Chrysler Corporation sponsored a competition for high-school students called the Plymouth Troubleshooting Contest. At the end of class one morning, our auto-shop teacher, Mr. Campbell, said to Tom and me, "I want to see you two guys after class this morning."

Oh no! Were we in trouble for not putting the tools away in their proper places? We wondered what he wanted of us.

He said, "Come on into my office, guys, and have a seat." He got right to the point. "The troubleshooting contest is around the corner, and I am asking the two of you to represent the Lakeview High School Auto Shop."

I couldn't believe what I was hearing. Oh my God! Me representing our high school? What an honor!

I said, "Are you sure, Mr. Campbell, that you want us to do this for our school?"

He said, "Yes, you will win the competition for Lakeview."

I immediately said I would gladly do this.

Tom looked at me, smiled and said to Mr. Campbell, "Me too! I will work with Frank."

How could this be? Autorama first, and now the prestige of being a participant in the troubleshooting contest? Wow! Hey, look at me—a student who was in the C group representing our high school in a national competition. Wow!

The purpose of the competition was to test our automotive skill level with accuracy and time. I had the fuel section, and Tom had the electrical. We practiced after school every day, including the night before the contest. Mr. Campbell was a fabulous coach, and he put his heart and soul into preparing us for the big day of the competition. His dedication to teaching us was second to none.

The competition consisted of diagnosing engine issues on a brand-new vehicle that Chrysler Corporation had recently introduced, the Plymouth Barracuda. This was a car designed to compete with the Ford Mustang and Chevrolet Camaro. The judging team would create identical electrical and fuel issues in each of the participants' cars. Teams of two had thirty minutes after the starting horn sounded to diagnosis, repair, test-drive, and then drive to the judging areas. So that we could practice, the Chrysler Corporation gave us the use of a car identical to the one on which we would be tested. We trained for weeks, putting in many long hours after school. Mr. Campbell would create an issue in the electrical or in the fuel system. He would say to us, "Ready, boys?"

"Yes!" we'd reply.

We watched him set the timer and say, "Go!"

Tom and I were intense, and there wasn't time to talk to each other because we were on a mission. We wanted to beat the clock and win this—hands down. Each time we practiced, we became faster and faster. We trained as if we were going to be in the Olympics. In our minds, this was more important than the Olympics. Winning this would go down in the history books forever! Frank and Tom, a couple of auto-shop students, would have their names on the Lakeview High School wall of fame. This would be our claim to fame— winning the 1967 Plymouth Troubleshooting Contest.

On the morning of the contest, I was ready to win and take home first prize. I had butterflies in my stomach, but deep down inside, I had a cocky but confident attitude. We could do this! I climbed up the three steps of that huge yellow school bus feeling the anticipation, not knowing what to expect, how many people would be there, or who would be watching us. I began to get nervous, but I didn't show it.

We were all quiet during our long, fifteen-mile ride down I-75 south. The trip seemed to take longer than it should have. However, we were all confident and ready to win this. The bus came to a screeching halt right in front Cobo Hall. Bleachers and grandstands were set up for the huge number of people cheering for their favorite teams. Mr. Campbell signed our team in, and we received our contest credentials, which were necessary to participate in this event.

On the public-address system, a loud voice said, "Good afternoon, ladies and gentlemen. Welcome to the Plymouth Troubleshooting Contest, sponsored by the Chrysler Corporation. Contestants, at the sound of the gun, begin. Good luck!"

We began to diagnose the problem with the engine. I found that the carburetor had been sabotaged and needed to be rebuilt. Tom found the ignition points were closed, and the timing was 180 degrees off. We fixed the issues and fired it up, turning the key, cranking the engine, and BAM! We had it running. It sounded great, and it appeared to be running within factory specifications. We closed the hood and drove it to the judges' stand for a final inspection.

The judges looked at the factory engine specifications and discovered we hadn't changed one of the incorrect spark plugs that had been installed in the number-four cylinder of that slant-six engine. Consequently, we came in third place out of three places to be awarded.

Tom felt horrible, but we had placed third in the state of Michigan. There were competitors who never did get their car finished—or even started. We held our heads up high and thanked Mr. Campbell for having enough confidence in us to ask us to represent our school. This was not only a proud moment for us. We also saw the glow of pride in Mr. Campbell's eyes. Tom and I didn't know at that time that by placing third in this competition, we would receive benefits after we had graduated from high school. Weeks before we were to walk down that aisle to receive our high school diplomas, we each received a Western Union Telegram from the Chrysler Corporation offering us positions within the company. We couldn't believe it.

Those positions were at the Chrysler world headquarters in Highland Park, Michigan. It was an unbelievable opportunity, even though I really wasn't a huge Chrysler product fan. I was still excited that I might be working for one of the biggest automobile manufacturers in the United States, one of what are known as the "Big Three" – General Motors, Ford and Chrysler. However, I needed to graduate from Lakeview High School first.

Thank you, Mr. Campbell for believing in us.

Would I Graduate?

There were two high-school career paths: one was designed for those who planned to attend college, and the other was for those who were going right into the world of work. You can guess the path that I chose. No college for this hands-on, C-student guy! Those of us who chose the world of work were able to enroll in co-op in our senior year of high school. One advantage of being in the co-op program was that our school day ended at noon. Many of us began our co-op jobs around 12:30 p.m. and worked until 11:00 p.m. I continued to work at D&W Standard throughout my high-school years, learning and improving my skills.

As well as being a high school senior, I was also in my fourth year at D&W, and promoted to the night-manager position. Everyone knew me and my 1964 Ford show car. I loved working for Ken and Ray. Many great memories were made there. My work and my car were the most important parts of my life. School was not that important to me. I sat through all of my academic classes, daydreaming and thinking about what I was going to do next with my car. Maybe change the gear ratio in the rear end or add another, bigger, more powerful carburetor setup.

Every now and then, a teacher like Mrs. Applebee would catch me daydreaming and would call out my name, saying, "Frank, are you paying attention?"

I would reply, "Yes, Mrs. Applebee. I am paying attention to you."

She then said, "Well then, come up to the chalkboard and diagram this sentence."

"Holy shit," I said to myself. "Diagram the sentence?" I took a wild guess from halfheartedly listening to her lesson and diagramed the sentence correctly.

She said to me in a stern voice, "Now go back to your seat and pay attention."

"Yes, Mrs. Applebee."

The school year was flying by, and now it was quickly coming to the end. Reality was setting in. I finally started to worry about my grades. Would I graduate? I needed to pass my government class to graduate. My approach to school was to lie low, not cause any trouble, and stay under the radar. I was satisfied with a C or D average. No one asked any questions of me, and it appeared no one really cared. As long as I didn't create any discipline problems, I was safe.

Remember, I was the student in the C group. I was not an academic achiever, nor was I a star athlete. I was just me. If I didn't graduate, I wasn't sure how I would be able to explain it. After all, what would everyone say and think? Oh, I came up with a few story lines: "I didn't graduate because I forgot to take gym class." Or, "The counselor lost all of my records when she traded in her car because the used car porter at the dealer threw them in the trash."

In those days, you received the actual diploma during the graduation ceremonies. Walking down that long aisle and onto the stage, your diploma was handed to you with a firm hand –shake from the Principal. Although we were allowed to attend the ceremony, that didn't guarantee I will be receiving the real deal....a diploma. The reason for this is the final exams and the final grades were posted days before the event. Graduation for me was pending on passing my government exam.

It was that simple. I arranged to meet with my government teacher to discuss my immediate problem: graduation. I thanked God my parents were not interested in my schoolwork. However, I would be in DEEP trouble if I didn't graduate. The Italians loved to talk among themselves and compare notes on who's doing what? If the news of me not graduating from high school got out, the Antonucci family name would be tarnished. I could visualize the big tune-up that would be heading my way.

During the meeting with my teacher, Mr. Portlance, I asked what I needed to do to pass his class. He said, "Frank, you will have to do the reading assignments and participate more in classroom discussions."

I said, "That's it?"

He said, "That's it."

Immediately, I asked one of my frat friends (Larry) for some help. Frats paid attention in class and did their homework and Larry was a former greaser-turned-frat. We arranged to meet, and I parked my car in the back of the Saint

Clair Shores Public Library. I didn't want to ruin my cool image by having someone see *me* at a library!

Larry showed me a way to take notes and gave me some recommendations on how to participate more in class. I told him what had happened in my tenth-grade algebra class with Ms. Kowalchak and how embarrassed I was and how I couldn't forget what the b—teacher had said to me.

Larry gave me few tips about what I needed to pass my government class. He said, "Frank, take time to read the chapter and participate in the daily lessons. Make the teacher feel like he is the most important part of your day. Read and review the homework assignments, and turn them in on time. Raise your hand, and most of all, pay attention in class. Frank, you're not stupid. You can do this. You are just not applying yourself. If you really want to graduate, get it together now."

I will never forget the advice Larry gave me that night at the library. We ended our conversation on this note. Larry told me, "I will help you pass your government class, but you have to at least make an effort on your own, participate in class and do the assignments."

That advice from Larry gave me a much-needed kick in the pants and ignited a fire in my backside. I began to take Mr. Portlance's government class very seriously. I was amazed at how much I didn't know about George Washington and the House of Representatives—unbelievable!

The weeks turned into days, and the buzz around the school was graduation. The exam schedules were posted on the bulletin boards, and the first exam that got my attention was my government exam. I choked up at the thought, but I believed I could pass it.

The date of the exam came, and it was now judgment day for me. I was either going to pass or fail. My Cuban heels clicked and I felt butterflies in my stomach as I walked down that long hallway to my final destination, Room 219.

I walked through the door and sat in my assigned seat. I was confident and determined that I would pass the exam that was standing in my way of graduating and freedom. Mr. Portlance was standing outside the door and said, "Good morning, Frank. Are you ready to pass the exam?" He spoke with a smirk on his face.

"Good morning. I am here to take your exam and pass it with flying colors." I told him. Then I said to myself, "Do not get too overconfident. Just take the exam and get the hell out of here. The teacher is holding your future in his hands. Be cool and keep quiet."

I needed my high-school diploma to be able to continue with my life. Besides, if I didn't graduate from high school, our family name would be ruined!

The exam was multiple choice, giving me some clues. However, as I read and reread each of the choices, my confidence wavered. Was it A or B or C or NONE OF THE ABOVE? I gave it all I had, did my best, and then, time was up.

"Class," he said, "put your pencils down and turn in your exams."

There were no more chances for me. I had run out of options. As we were leaving the class, we said good-bye to our teacher. My classmates stood in the hallway asking one another, "How did you do?"

Some said, "That was a breeze. I am glad I studied and took notes. They really came in handy."

Sheepishly I said, "Yeah, me too." But I thought, "Notes? I was too busy building a show car. Why do I need to know about government and economics anyway? I don't need that to work on cars."

However, my show car and trophy wouldn't help me graduate from high school. My education might not be a priority to me, but I needed to graduate.

The day came—graduation. Saturday, June 15, 1967. There were no more chances, no more homework, and soon, no more school (I hoped). We assembled in alphabetical order on the football field. I had never before stepped one foot on that green football field. The janitors (custodians) covered the path that we were to walk on with a huge gray canvas mat. With the number of graduates and spectators on the field, walking without those mats would cause damage to the turf that would take months to repair. Sometimes I thought that the football field was more important to the school than our auto shop—and it was.

The sun was shining bright, and there was not a cloud in the sky. The fresh air coming off the lake was awesome. The high-school band played "Pomp and Circumstance." The teaching staff made sure we were all lined up perfectly. Mrs. Applebee said in a loud, clear voice, "Students! Be sure to hand your three-by-five cards to Mr. Black. Do not get out of line."

As the band finished playing, our principal said in a loud, commanding voice, "Graduates, please be seated." He said a few words, and then our class president said some parting words. I didn't remember a thing that was said. As my heart pounded though my graduation gown, I wondered if anyone could hear it. I didn't know whether I had passed my government exam or failed it. Would I be attending summer school or graduating? The suspense was beginning to show as the sweat ran down my face.

Then the principal announced, "At this time, we will begin to distribute your diplomas. As you hear your name, come up to the stage. Then exit to your right and take your seat." I felt my stomach get queasy. We were called up in alphabetical order, and soon I heard, "Francis Joseph Antonucci." I walked up the center aisle toward the stage. My knees trembled, and I began to sweat profusely. This was it—no more stories, no more BS. I was at the end of the line. I received a firm handshake. I didn't know if this meant good luck or good riddance. Then I was handed what appeared to be my diploma. As I walked back to my seat, I opened the diploma and saw my name printed on the certificate. Wow! I *had* graduated from high school. *I had made it!* I was now a high-school graduate. Good-bye to school forever— or so I thought.

Saying Good-By to D&W

My knowledge in the automotive mechanics field had expanded. I was seventeen years old and doing brake jobs, head gaskets, exhaust systems, and removing and replacing transmissions and engines. I still loved the everyday challenges of my job.

My workday also included managing the working staff, balancing the incoming cash and scheduling the daily workload. Ken and Ray had purchased a gas station in the local boat marina and were rarely at the Standard station on the corner of Harper and Erben Street. I had started out as a helper, and now I was in charge of the employees and the midday shift until closing time. I was making great money, and every time my responsibilities increased, I felt important. I had accomplished many tasks throughout my years working there. I simply loved working for those two guys, and we made many good memories and had great times. I truly enjoyed my job. However, I really wanted to become an auto-body man. In those days, we were called *bump men*. I wanted to be the best there was and not second best.

In our world, recognition is always offered to those students who have above-average GPAs or students with athletic capabilities. If you were a C student and didn't play sports, you were a nobody, and you were written off and not recognized. This continues to be the trend in today's world—just take a look in the media. I wanted to be someone who would obtain recognition for doing auto-body work that could be seen. When I installed a transmission or did a tune-up on someone's car, you couldn't see what I had done because it was hidden under the hood. I felt a great deal of gratification when I heard my name called for the visible hard work I put into my show car. I loved all the compliments and accolades from everyone who saw it. I wanted and needed– that to continue in my life. I wanted to reach for more.

At seventeen years of age, fresh out of high school, I didn't know what my future had in store. However, to explore my future meant saying good-bye to Ken and Ray. I thought about it over and over. "What am I going to say to the two guys who gave me everything I needed to succeed?" I felt I was betraying them, but I couldn't put it off any longer. Ken had asked me earlier that week, "Is everything OK?"

"Yeah, Ken," I answered, but now I couldn't wait any longer. So I arranged to have a meeting with the two of them on Friday of that same week. They wore expressions of concern.

Ken said, "What's wrong, Frankie?"

I said, "I want to thank you guys for everything you have done for me and given me these past four years. I couldn't have done any of this without your help. I learned so much here, and you gave me the confidence I needed so badly. But I really want to become a body man. I want to do more with my hands and do collision work." I took a deep breath and went on to say, "Please don't misunderstand me. I've loved my work here but I want to work on wrecks. I am giving you my two-week notice and moving on."

I began to tear up with sadness and apprehension about leaving and beginning a new career. They supported my decision, and they reflected and complimented me on the outstanding job I had done while working for them. They also busted my balls for the some of the mistakes I had made and the money I had cost them. We had a few laughs and parted as friends.

Ray passed a number of years after I left the station, but I continue to see Ken a few times a year. It is always nice to see and talk to him and reminisce about the old days. I will never forget them.

Thank you, Ray Dixon and Ken Wall.

Recommendations and Decisions

I relished the fact that I was now a high-school graduate—free as a bird, free to come and go as I pleased. My whole future was before me. I was the king, and nobody was going to tell me what to do. I kept answering the same old question: "Frank, what are you going to do now that you're out of high school?"

I always responded with the same words. "I am not sure."

My uncles would say, "You need to work in the factory. It offers security and benefits too." I realized their intentions were good. However, working in the factory was the last thing I wanted to do with my life. Most of the men in the tri-county metropolitan Detroit area worked for the Big Three.

I knew, deep down inside, I wanted to be an auto-body man instead and the best one around, with a good reputation within the trade. I just wanted to work on cars.

My parents wanted me to be a tool and die maker like my good buddy Johnny's dad. They would say, "Be a tool and die maker like Mr. Parinno." I never said no to my parents, at least out loud. I would say it under my breath many times. The tool and die trade was as boring to me as sitting in my government class. Not for me. Day after day, I heard these words from my mom: "I talked to Johnny's mom, and she said that her husband can arrange for you to take the apprenticeship test."

Just hearing the word *test* made my skin crawl. I thought, "Don't all you people get it? Ever since I purchased my paper route at ten years of age, you haven't been involved in my life. While I was in school, you didn't attend any conferences, talk to me about my grades, look at my homework—you just weren't involved. As long as I stayed out of trouble, I was OK. Furthermore, I built a show car, and you never asked where the money was coming from, and NOW you want to get involved in my future. No thanks."

Yet, I just couldn't just say no to my parents. I still craved their approval and much-needed love. Maybe this time I would receive their approval, if I agreed to take the apprenticeship test. The testing site was in the skilled-trades building, which was located in the heart of downtown Detroit. The test was scheduled on a Monday at 10:00 a.m., and the testing area was on the twelfth floor.

I went up to the twelfth floor. As I looked out the window, I saw my car parked on Woodward Street facing north with the top down. I'd rather be cruising than here, I thought. After I had graduated, I sold my 1964 Galaxy XL show car and purchased a 1964 Chevrolet Corvette convertible 327—a four-speed with a medium metallic-blue exterior and a navy-blue interior. I loved to drive it around with the top down and feel my thick dark-brown hair blowing in the wind. I was still being a cool dude with a cool car.

Example of my 1964 Corvette convertible

I sighed and was thinking I was here to take a test instead. I received my test and a sharp number-two pencil for writing down my answers. The entire test was made up of fifty questions, and I didn't care a bit about my score.

All I knew was that I was satisfying my parents' request. I didn't want to work in a tool and die shop. When I finished, I handed the facilitator my test and the number-two pencil. He informed me I would have the results within the week. He went on to say that I might want to try calling them in a few days for my results.

I said, "Thank you." The elevator ride was smooth and quick. As I exited the building, I saw my Corvette just sitting there, parked and waiting to be fired up and driven. I inserted the key into the ignition and pushed in the clutch with my left foot. With my right foot on the gas pedal, I put that four-speed into first gear and began to cruise back to Saint Clair Shores. After I got home, I said to my mom, "I took the test this morning."

She said, "That's nice."

That was it. "That's nice." I waited a few days with anticipation and curiosity and then made the phone call to get my test results.

"Skilled-trade testing center," the man on the other end of the line said.

"Hello, my name is Frank Antonucci, and I was curious about my test results."

I was very pleased to hear his words. He said, "Frank, unfortunately, your test score was too low." He went on to say that I could retake the test in six months.

I thanked him, and that was the end of that idea. My parents never brought it up to me again. My uncles kept it up, though. They wanted me to work for Chrysler Corporation.

"Frank," they said, "if you are not planning on attending college, the Big Three have benefits and job security."

Little did we know how much that would change in the future. I would nod my head in agreement, but I only did it to be respectful to my uncles. I knew what I wanted, and I was going for it.

Back in the day, to get a break in the collision business, you had to know someone to get hired. My experience building a show car didn't mean a thing to potential employers. It was like I was trying to join a secret organization, and I couldn't get in. When I talked with a prospective employer about the experience I had doing bodywork on my own, he looked at me as if I were a storyteller and a punk kid who was nothing but a wannabe body man.

Then I remembered year's earlier meeting one of my dad's buddies. They worked together at a Michigan Consolidated Gas company substation. The substation was located on Jefferson Avenue, just a stone's throw away from Belle Island, a family hot spot where we had picnics and barbeques on Sundays. The people who lived near the island enjoyed riding their bicycles or walking around the park enjoying the summer's breeze.

I was thirteen years old when my dad said, "Hop in the car. We're going for a ride." He wanted to go over and see his good buddy named Frank Mini. As we walked up his driveway, we noticed the garage door was open. I saw Frank repairing a huge dent on a front fender from a 1940 Ford coupe. The reason we were going over to Frank's house was to talk to Frank about repairing our family's 1962 Ford that I had previously customized. Someone had put a softball-sized dent into the right rear quarter panel, and my dad asked Frank to fix and paint it. I watched Frank use a special hammer and a block of steel to slowly restore the shape of the panel.

Pick-Hammer   *Multi-Purpose Dolly*

My eyes were glued to Frank every time he struck the panel with his hammer and used the block of steel for support. I couldn't believe my eyes. Frank was doing bodywork. One day I would be like Frank, I decided: a body man. And I would become the best! My dad didn't see much of Frank after that because he had quit working for Michigan Consolidated Gas and opened up his own collision shop with his partner, Jimmy Robinson. Their shop was R&M Collision, and it was located on Nine Mile Road in East Detroit, Michigan. Now, I was fresh out of high school, seventeen years old, and my future was not locked in stone. However, I knew I wanted to do collision work, and I just needed that lucky break. So I drove over to Frank's shop and asked him for a job. At first, he laughed and said, "Frankie, this is a rough trade to get into." He went on to say, "Things are slow, and I couldn't afford to hire you full time."

I said, "I will work for you for free. I just want to learn the trade."

"OK, bring your tools, and I will see you tomorrow."

I didn't have many tools or a big fancy toolbox. My box consisted of a small, hand-carried, gray two-drawer

Craftsman toolbox. I remember walking into the shop, and the guys couldn't hold back the laughter. One of them said to me, "Hey, kid! Do you need any help carrying your tools?"

Example of my first tool box

Everyone was laughing along with him, but this didn't stop me. I was on a mission and wanted to learn the trade. Frank was well known for his metal finishing and lead work. He was quiet and didn't say much. As I worked, he would walk by and tell me what needed to be worked on and then let me do it on my own. But when things didn't go right with whatever he saw being worked on in the shop, we all ran for cover. Frank would blow up like a can of spray paint placed on an open fire. At those times, Frank became unapproachable, and no one dared to say anything to him.

Frank took me under his wing and taught me the basics of auto-body repair, which stayed with me for the rest of my life. Frank could be cantankerous at times, but he was a great teacher. I was finally working in a full-fledged body shop, proudly wearing a uniform identifying me as an employee of R&M Collision. The sweet smell of paint and body fillers filled the air as I walked through the front door of the shop. Oh, those memories!

I worked for Frank for a few months, and then I received a phone call from a guy who knew I was trying to break into the scene. This man's name was Dave Lester. He said, "How would you like to work at the Corvette shop?"

I said, "The 'Vette shop? Are you kidding me?"

Everyone who was anyone wanted to work at the Corvette shop – a dream job! I thought about that California sound, great tunes like "California Dreaming," by the Mamas and Papas, or the music of the Beach Boys—and how about Jan and Dean? This was 1967, the summer of love, and I could be a part of it.

The offer I received from the Corvette shop was one I couldn't turn down. It was a full-time position—forty hours a week—and the salary was unbelievable. I couldn't pass up this opportunity. I gave Frank my notice. He was not happy; he felt betrayed, but I was immature at that time, and was only thinking about myself. Later on in life, this would be a lesson I wouldn't forget.

I began working at the Corvette shop the very next day. Wow! All the cool Corvettes! I was Mr. Big Stuff and beginning to expand my career. The owner and manager's name was Ed Lare. They all called me by the nickname my dad had given me earlier as a little boy: Skip.

This was another new experience that I added to my sponge-like brain. I couldn't absorb enough. I was learning more and more every day. I initially was hired to wet sand and rub out the freshly painted 'Vettes Dave had painted.

In those days, General Motors Corporation painted all of their vehicles with a lacquer-based paint. Several coats were applied by a professional painter and air-dried overnight. The next morning, the complete car would have to be wet sanded to remove all of the airborne dirt and bugs that might have landed in the topcoat. This process took up to four hours, using a bucket of water and six-hundred-grit sandpaper. The entire vehicle was wet sanded to remove the dirt and orange peel in the paint. Orange peel is a texture that appears in the paint that resembles the outer skin of an orange. That's how that term originated.

Example of wet sanding a Corvette

After the vehicle was thoroughly wet sanded and double-checked for orange peel, the next step was to use a high-speed polisher with a clean wool pad and, of course, the super duty rubbing compound. The objective was to remove all of the six-hundred-grit sanding scratches with the use of the wool pad and the super duty compound. The term often used for this process was "rubbing out the finish." Therefore, my new job description was "rub-out boy." This was the lowest of the low and a job no one wanted to do. Think of it like this. There's the chef, who cooks and prepares a fine meal, and then there's the person assigned to clean up after the chef, making the chef appear even greater. That was me, the clean-up guy. I didn't mind doing this. After all, I was learning and getting paid to learn—not bad!

I began wet sanding one Corvette a day and soon began to do two and three. I knew I wouldn't be doing this permanently, and I wanted to prove to everyone in the shop that I was not your average rub-out boy. As I finished wet sanding one Corvette, I would begin another. Each of the completed wet-sanded Corvettes mirrored a show-car finish, especially the darker-colored paint jobs. I took pride in hearing the guys say, "Nice job, Skip!"

I started out as a rub-out boy, and within three weeks, Ed called me into the office for a chat. He said, "I see a great deal of potential in you and a desire to learn. How would you like to be taught how to repair these 'Vettes?"

I said, "Wow, will you train me?"

He said yes. He went on to say, "I want to show you how to write an estimate of repairs." This was a major breakthrough for me, and my career began to elevate. Ed took me under his wing, and my rub-out boy days were behind me. Ed had hired my replacement.

Ed taught me the differences between the different fiberglass composites. He taught me what to use and how to use it. My first big repair job was to hang a new front end on a sunflower-yellow 1967 coupe. The front end was heavily damaged and in need of a total replacement. Before I began to work on the front end replacement, Ed sat me down in his office and taught me how to read a Mitchell's Collision Manual. Mitchell's was and still is the bible of the collision repair business, and it is still being used today. Of course, with today's modern technology, all of the information is located online. Approximately two months after I began working at the Vette shop, I was placed on commission. I was no longer receiving hourly compensation for my work. I had moved up to the big time. Ed asked me if I wanted to write estimates in addition to repairing those cool Corvettes.

I immediately said, "Yes."

He then said I would receive 50 percent of the repair labor and an additional fifty dollars a week for answering the phone and writing the estimates. I was rolling in cash and working twelve to fourteen hours a day. The more Corvettes I fixed, the more cash I made. I couldn't spend my money fast enough. My paychecks ranged from a low of $300 to a high of $600 per week. In 1967 and 1968, that was a huge amount of money to be making. I thought, who needs the factory, and who needs to attend college! Look at me now, Mrs. Applebee. I couldn't believe it, and I wanted to shout, "Look at me! I was a C student and did not go to college. And life is great."

I had the world by the tail. I was beating the system and all of the naysayers, too.

The Detroit Riots and Vietnam

Summer was over, 1967 was coming to an end, and it was a busy year for me. It was the last year for the Corvette Stingray as we knew it—good-bye to the spilt-window body style.

1967 Detroit Riots
Image: Howard Bingham/The LIFE Picture Collection/Getty, online: Cris Wild: Remembering the Detroit Riots of 1967

Then the infamous Detroit riots broke out in late summer, leaving the metropolitan Detroit area in a state of chaos and flames. We couldn't quite understand how this could be happening. It was the summer of love!

Detroit was approximately twenty miles south of Saint Clair Shores, and we could see smoke in the air from the fires. After dinner, our family crowded around our twenty-inch black-and-white console television and watched the nightly news programs. There were video clips of the fires and the looting. There were screaming people in the streets. I remember my dad telling my sister and me, "I don't want you kids going past Eight Mile Road." Eight Mile Road was the northern Detroit city line.

"OK, Dad," we said.

I hopped in my car and drove over to my good friend Joe's house, and away we went—straight to Detroit to see what was going on. We thought we were invincible, and at that age, we probably were—untouchable, too. Joe and I wanted a closer look at the Detroit riots. As we approached Eight Mile Road, on the Detroit side, it looked as if the Army National Guard had invaded the city. There were soldiers

91

carrying M-16 rifles locked and loaded, and they were ready to prevent any more fires and looting. Huge military tanks moved up and down Eight Mile. It looked like a scene out of a war movie, but was real, not a movie. Many lives were lost and buildings were burned to the ground. I don't believe Detroit ever recovered from this atrocity.

After the news coverage of the Detroit riots, the media shifted focus to the war in Vietnam. The war was beginning to escalate, and it seemed there was no end in sight. The cameras showed the many body bags that were being shipped home with our friends, brothers, sons, and daughters inside. There were a great number of people who protested the war locally and nationally as well. The voices were loud and clear: "Get us out of Vietnam." I knew I was destined to either be drafted or enlist in the military. It was a decision that only I could make. I had a steady girlfriend, and we'd been together four years. I was making good money, and I had been promoted to assistant manager of the Corvette shop. Yet I knew I couldn't watch everyone go to war and sit back and do nothing. I had to make a decision soon.

Enlisting in the Army National Guard

1968

In February, I turned eighteen, so I made the decision to enlist in the Army National Guard. I wanted to do my part to serve our country. This meant that I had to quit my job at the Corvette shop. I will admit I was scared out of my pants and didn't know what to expect, but I found out quickly what was meant by the old song and movie: "You're in The Army Now!"

I was assigned to the 182nd Artillery unit based out of Southfield, Michigan. The National Guard requirements were that enlisted men had to be on active duty[9] for a period of six months, and upon returning to our home unit, we had to attend a weekend monthly meeting and participate in a two-week summer training at Camp Grayling for a period of six years. Camp Grayling is located in the northern part of Michigan's Lower Peninsula.

Here I was, the oldest boy in an Italian American family, a guy who had never been away from home or away from my mamma and papa. I wondered how this would work and what to expect. I didn't know what the Army had in store for me. Whoa, was I surprised!

Basic training was intense. I was in reasonably good shape, in good physical condition. I was a strong, fit young man – so I thought. I remembered my experiences in my ninth-grade physical education class. It had not been one of my favorite subjects. But now I was a full-grown man of eighteen who worked hard with his whole body, and I knew it all…and then some.

My dad drove me to Detroit Metropolitan Airport for my flight to boot camp. The plane landed two hours later, and we were directed to board the big olive-green Army bus that was waiting to take us to our final destination. The Army instructed us not to bring many personal items. "We will supply you with everything you will need," they said.

Every seat on the bus was taken. Approximately fifty new recruits sat quietly during the fifty-mile trip. We

[9] A person who is active duty is in the military full time. They work for the military full time, may live on a military base, and can be deployed at any time.

approached a sign that read **WELCOME TO FORT CAMPBELL, HOME OF THE 101ST AIRBORNE DIVISION.** In a loud voice, a man wearing a hat that looked like something Smokey the Bear might wear shouted, "GET OFF THE BUS, YOU RUM DUMBS!"

I was scared shitless. *Rum dumbs*? Was he talking to me?

Army Drill Sargent

"LINE UP, YOU RECRUITS! WE ARE GOIN' TO MAKE YOU WAR MACHINES! I AM DRILL SERGEANT JONES. YOUR ASS IS GRASS, AND I AM THE POWER LAWNMOWER."

We then were ordered to march quickly over to the reception station, where we were processed for the next seven days. We were given our GI-style haircuts, uniforms, shots, and aptitude tests, and we were indoctrinated into the US Army. We waited patiently, anticipating where our barracks would be. We could hear in the near distance the sound of that trumpet blasting out that most recognizable tune: Reveille.[10]

---

[10] *Reveille* is a bugle call, trumpet call, or pipes call most often associated with the military and prisons; it is chiefly used to wake military personnel and prisoners at sunrise. The name comes from *réveille* (or *réveil*), the French word

After the trumpet stopped playing, the Drill Sergeant entered the barracks and said in a loud and crystal-clear voice, "TIME TO WAKE UP, YOU MAGGOTS! YOU WILL BE RUNNING OVER TO YOUR PERMANANENT BARRACKS! LET'S GO, TURDS!"

Upon entering the barracks, I noticed the latrine on my left, and I didn't see any privacy walls in between the commodes. I thought, "That's strange." I had never gone number two without closing and securing the door. I needed my privacy. After we were all settled in and our personal belongings were neatly placed into our footlockers, we heard this loud voice say, "Fall out, you lousy maggots. Today you will begin your training."

We ran over to the Physical Training area A.K.A. the PT field and were instructed to run one mile. "GET MOVING, MAGGOTS!" My lack of physical stamina began to show immediately. I ran the track one time around and thought that was a mile. I really didn't know I needed to run three more times around the track to equal a mile. I saw the guys in my platoon huffing and puffing, and I thought how glad I was that I was not a smoker. I felt pretty good.

The Drill Sergeant came up to me and said, "What the hell are you doing, soldier? Why have you stopped running?"

I said, "I am all finished. I ran my mile."

The Drill Sergeant looked as if he was going to kill me for being a smartass. I ran far past the four required laps that

for "wake up." British Army Cavalry and Royal Horse Artillery regiments sound a call. In modern times, the US military plays (or sounds) "reveille" in the morning. Some unofficial lyrics are *"You've got to get up, You've got to get up, You've got to get up this morning . . ."*

day, and I never again assumed that I knew what was going on with physical training exercises. The Drill Sergeant made an example out of me that day. I soon realized I was not in a John Wayne movie. This was the real thing. I was in the Army now.

I became more and more familiar with the daily routine commonly known as PT, and I began to get used to my new army lifestyle. My muscles developed and my endurance increased from the daily crucial PT training. I was becoming leaner and trimmer by the day.

Graduation from basic training was on the horizon, and I had acclimated to the army protocol. However, after approximately two weeks, I still had not gone number two. As I walked by the latrine, I would see the guys reading the newspaper and talking to one another while sitting on the commode. Yikes! Not me! Then one day after lunch, all hell broke loose. It was either use the latrine or change myself. I wouldn't have cared if I had been at home plate during the Detroit Tigers World Series. I used the latrine and lost my inhibitions that day. I said to myself that I was now a certified army soldier.

The day finally came, and it was time to graduate from basic training. Hooray! As I looked into the mirror and admired my new appearance, I couldn't believe it. I had been transformed into a lean, mean fighting machine. I ran the mile without any issues and kept up with the best of them. After I graduated from boot camp, we received our orders, telling us where we would be sent for additional training. I was sent to Fort Sill in Oklahoma to artillery school for ten weeks. My assignment was to drive a two-and-a-half-ton four-by-four troop carrier commonly known as a "deuce and a half."

Driving this monster truck didn't compare to my 1964 Ford Galaxy or my Corvette convertible. This heavy off-road truck carried up to 100,000 pounds of troops and artillery equipment with a top speed of about 50 mph. I certainly couldn't pop the clutch or spin the wheels.

Deuce Truck

I signed out the "deuce" in the morning, picked up the 155 Howitzer, and loaded up the troops. My orders were to drive out to the firing range every day. After I parked and camouflaged the truck, I was training with the rest of my squad. In the meantime, back home, the Tigers had won the World Series. That must have been exciting to see.

Also in the fall of 1968, we were anticipating the new car lineup. In those days, the Big Three changed the body styles every year. It was a real treat to run down to the local new-car dealers and sneak a peek behind the secret locations, seeing the new car line-up in advance.

We were in awe of the dramatic changes being made by the Motor City designers. This was when the words *emissions, clean air,* and *pollution* became popular buzzwords from the federal government. The Environmental Protection Agency or EPA was proposed by President

Richard Nixon and began operation on December 2, 1970, after Nixon signed an executive order.

The EPA was closing in at the Big Three auto companies and in full force. There were many conversations in hot-rod circles and among car guys, wondering what would happen to all of our high-performance cars. In 1968, the feds mandated all 1968 vehicles should produce cleaner air, and therefore emissions controls were installed on every new vehicle. This was the beginning of the end for high-performance vehicles as we knew them.

I also received a Dear John letter from home. My girlfriend of four years had left me for someone new, but what could I do? Not much. I was in the army, and I had to suck it up and move on. All I could say was it was over.

I began to adjust more and more to the military lifestyle and began to consider leaving the Army National Guard and transferring into the regular army. I contacted the necessary personnel to do the transfer into the army, which would mean I'd go over to and fight alongside with my buddies with whom I had been training for the past five months. I was informed I would have to return to Detroit and be released from my National Guard unit, and then I would be reassigned and sent to Vietnam. I agreed. My mind was made up to go and fight.

As the plane was landing and I saw the towers and stacks of the Ford Motor Company, I began to think about my roots: fast cool cars, the Corvette shop, and eating submarine sandwiches. A close friend of mine was there to pick me from the airport. His name was Mike, but we called him Meatloaf. He was driving his 1967 lime-green GT Mustang fastback equipped with a four-speed, 390 cubic-inch engine. This car was quick and bad to the bone.

Example of Meatloaf's 1967 Ford Mustang GT 390 4speed
By Sicnag (1967 Ford Mustang GT Fastback) [CC BY 2.0
(http://creativecommons.org/licenses/by/2.0)]

On our way back to Saint Clair Shores, we made a few stops along the way. I soon became reconnected to civilian life. I didn't have to choose between cars and the Army —my transfer request was denied in Oklahoma.

Many years have passed since my days in basic training. It is in our nature to remember the good times and try to forget the bad times. I was fortunate that my life was spared, that I did not simply become a wartime statistic, returning home with a limb missing or a lifelong disability known as posttraumatic stress disorder (PTSD).

I listen to war veteran's talk about PTSD but couldn't relate or make a connection with this disorder. I heard them talk about having flashbacks. Years later, in 1987, film director Stanley Kubrick came out with a movie called *Full Metal Jacket*. As I sat there watching this movie with my wife, Chris, I became very quiet and withdrawn.

Chris asked me, "What's wrong?"

I said, "I finally can connect with these veterans who have returned from war because this movie is exactly how it was for me in basic training."

I couldn't believe what I saw and felt from reliving that part of the movie regarding the time I spent in basic training. During those first thirty-five minutes, had an immediate flashback to basic training. The accuracy of the film's depiction was incredible and surreal. I felt a lump in my throat as I thought about all of those who had served so bravely and sacrificed so much for our country.

I felt guilty for a long time because I had only thought of myself and chose not to join the regular army and fight the war in Vietnam with my buddies. Now, I am OK with it and no longer feel guilty. I know God saved my life for a purpose that came clear only later on in my life.

Thank you to all of you, past and present, who made that almighty sacrifice and fought for our country.

Readjusting to Civilian Life

As 1968 came to an end, I looked forward to beginning 1969, a new year, a time to start over. I knew I needed to return to the reality of working in the body shop. I drove over to the Corvette shop hoping to resume the great and exciting career I had prior to leaving for the army.

I walked through the front door and saw many new faces I didn't recognize. I was greeted by a man who was sitting in Ed's office. He said, "Can I help you?"

I said, "Where's Ed?"

He said, "Ed?"

I said, "Yes, Ed. The manager who ran this shop."

"Who are you?"

I said, "My name is Skip Antonucci. I was Ed's assistant manager before I left for active duty in the army. I want to return to my old job."

He said, "We don't have an opening for you here any longer."

I was pissed off and upset that my job was gone. I asked, "Where are my tools?"

He said, "We didn't know whose tools were whose, so we stored them in the paint room and covered them up with cardboard." The current manager's name was Tim. He said, "Ed left because of a long-term incurable sickness he has." I tried to connect with Ed for closure, but I never saw or talked to him again.

That day, as I walked through the shop to pick up my tools and personal belongings, I saw many changes had taken place. The counterculture had taken over. A strong smell of marijuana filled the air, and the acid rock music playing loudly in the shop was a message to me. A guy like me, fresh out of basic training with a neat army-style haircut, wouldn't fit in. There was one longhair who was a war protester, and the comments he was making were directed to me as I rolled out my huge Snap-On toolbox. I said to myself, "Stop bitching and join the army. See what being a man all is about."

The longhairs knew I wouldn't fit into that lifestyle. The format of the shop had changed direction, and I didn't want to place myself in a situation that would not be productive for me.

Here I was, crushed and rejected all over again, just when I thought I would be making a name for myself in the collision field. I was out of a job and had to start all over

101

again. I was still only eighteen, so many old-timers who worked in the body shops wouldn't even think of giving me a start in their shops to prove myself.

I couldn't go back to work for Frank Mini at R&M Collision. Frank had given me my start and had the confidence in me that one day I would be an outstanding body man. I had been too immature and cocky to understand the opportunity he had given me. It was all about me and no one else. I received a better offer and left him flat. I didn't even give him a chance to teach me. I remember the hurt look in his eyes when I said I was leaving—as if he took it personally.

Later on in life, Frank told me he was crushed when I gave him my notice. Although I had only worked for him for a short period of time, I learned from him the basic fundamentals of being a body man—and not just a body man, but an excellent body man. Today Frank and I are very close friends.

Thank you, Frank.

Starting Over

I received a Western Union telegram[11] from the Chrysler Corporation in the beginning of December of 1968. Remember that Tom and I had placed third in the Plymouth Troubleshooting competition? I immediately opened the telegram, and it read, "Chrysler Corporation World Headquarters is interested in hiring you for a position located in Highland Park, Michigan. Dial the number listed on the bottom of this page and make an appointment with personnel for an interview within the next three business days."

I dialed the number and made my appointment with the personnel department. I carefully and nervously wrote down all of the instructions I was given by the woman making the appointment. She said, "Do you have any questions for me, Mr. Antonucci?"

I said, "No, ma'am. Thank you, ma'am."

After the conversation ended, I went into my closet and took out my suit, white shirt, and tie. I wanted to look my best for my interview, and this would require wearing my Sunday best. There were two positions available for me. The first position was working in the design studio as an apprentice clay-model maker, and the second position was working in the plastics and rubber laboratory. I hoped to work in the clay-model studio because it would enable me to utilize the skills I had learned in the body shop. I enjoyed working with my hands, and I was familiar with the different sizes and shapes of the contoured auto bodies. Sculpturing

---

[11] The Western Union Company is an American financial services and communications company. Up until it discontinued the service in 2006, Western Union was the best-known US Company in the business of exchanging telegrams.

clay is similar to surfacing and repairing a damaged fender. I believed my experiences in applying and sanding Bondo and fiberglass would give me an advantage during my interview. I might soon be employed by the Chrysler Corporation, so this might be the big break I needed, my chance to work for one of the Big Three.

A week before my big interview, I made a clay model. One of my army buddies was employed at General Motors and was already a skilled clay-model maker. His name was Dean, and I asked him if he would give me a quick lesson to prepare me for my interview. I also asked him for his guidance in building a one-eighteenth scale clay model for my interview. Dean gladly accepted my invitation and brought over the clay-modeling tools he used daily in the styling department. I was sure that bringing a visual example of what I could do with my hands to the interview would secure that position for me.

The big day was only minutes away. Was this the moment that would decide my future? As I waited, I hoped the sweat dripping down from my undershirt would not show as my heart pounded profusely.

I heard these words: "Mr. Antonucci? Mr. Bettiga will see you now."

I introduced myself with a firm handshake. He said in a resolute voice, "Have a seat, young man." There was a strong smell of nicotine in the air, and I noticed his ashtray was full of cigarette butts. I watched him as he read my brief résumé. For the first time ever, I wished I had paid attention in Mrs. Applebee's English class. I briefly remembered the week we were doing employment applications and résumés. I had spent the time thinking about building my show car.

He looked at my clay model; however, I wasn't sure whether it was a hit or a miss. I remember him saying, "Hmm. Looks nice…did you build this?"

I replied, "Yes sir."

"Do you have any questions for me, Frank?"

I replied, "Do I have the job?"

He said, "I will give you a call within the next few days."

"Thank you for your time and giving me the opportunity to work for Chrysler." I picked up my clay model and said good-bye to his secretary. Then I hopped into my car and drove back to Saint Clair Shores. All the way home, I wondered if I had made the cut. I wished I had paid more attention in my academic classes. Maybe everyone was right—I was still in the C group and didn't belong at a company as big as the Chrysler Corporation.

I waited patiently for that phone call from Mr. Bettiga. We didn't have cell phones or computers in the sixties. Our only means of communication was the house telephone. My mom, who usually sat in her favorite chair either talking on the phone or answering the phone, picked it up when it rang. I heard her say, "He's upstairs. I will get him for you. Just a moment, please." She called up, "Frankie, this call is for you."

I ran downstairs and said, "Hello?"

On the other end, the person said, "This is Mr. Bettiga, and I am calling to talk to you about the interview. This is what is going on. The apprentice clay-modeling position has not been decided, and we will not be making that decision for a few more weeks. We cannot guarantee that position to you, and you may or may not be hired for it. However, we do have a guaranteed position beginning immediately working as a lab technician in the plastic and rubber laboratory."

I thought about it and accepted the job I was offered. I didn't want to take a gamble and end up with no job. The job required me to wear a dress shirt and tie and dress slacks. This was the daily dress code. I had my own desk and phone. I thought I was a big shot! I worked with a team of twelve engineers and four other technicians. Our building and department was located in the heart of Chrysler's world headquarters. We were in the same building that performed, developed, and tested the designs and innovations that would be featured in future Chrysler vehicles. I met the man who designed the famous Pistol Grip 4-speed shifter. His name was Bruce and his shifter was replicated from a 45 caliber pistol. I watched it begin as a sketch on a piece of loose-leaf paper, and final become reality. How cool was this?

1970 Dodge Challenger RT
By Sicnag (1970 Dodge Challenger RT 426 Hemi) [CC BY 2.0
http://creativecommons.org/licenses/by/2.0)]

My job was testing foam rubber composite and vinyl materials. BORING! I wasn't used to being in an office for eight hours a day with about two hours of work to do and then sitting there for the next six hours just trying to look busy. I saw people reading books, playing card games, and reading the daily newspaper. What kind of company hires someone for a forty-hour workweek and only has ten hours of work for them to do? This was not my idea of how to be a good employee. It just didn't fit into my work ethic. Chrysler was noted back in the day for hiring and laying off people before they were able to make their first year of seniority. In November of 1969, I received my layoff notice. I was relieved to have an excuse to leave that job, and I hoped never to return to Highland Park. That was the end of that "good job."

College, the Second Time Around

I began to think about my future and decided to return to college. The first time I had enrolled into college was September of 1967, when I was fresh out of high school. I did it to please everyone except myself. I didn't have any interest in college, and my actions exemplified it. I acted like a young punk kid who was an immature know-it-all. I made a fool out of myself. I was enrolled in a political science class and didn't like the professor because he had a long beard and long hair, and he reminded me of a war protester. Week after week, we would sit in his class, and I would say to myself, "Who does this guy think he is? What is he was teaching us? Garbage?" I was in college and paying for it myself. I wasn't about to let some hippie war protester tell me what to do. My classmates used to talk about him after class, and then one day, a few students said they believed he was teaching us communism. That was all I needed to hear, and that spurred me to tell him what I thought of him. Toward the end of that semester, I walked up to him and said, "I think you're a commie and trying to brainwash your class. I am putting you on notice. I quit!"

Looking back at that day, I realize now I made a huge fool of myself. That was another day that I will never forget. I would hear these words over and over again: "In the future, you will need a college education to get a good job." Deep down inside, I knew that advice was correct, but I didn't want to hear it because I was afraid of failing. The stigma of being in the C group still haunted me, and I couldn't get past it. The thought of not measuring up and being laughed at would never happen to me again. I didn't have much confidence in high school. How was I ever going to succeed in college?

In the late summer of 1969, I once again enrolled in classes at the local community college, and this time I was determined to complete two semesters. I wanted to be a completer and not a dropout. I wasn't going to give up on myself. After all, the army taught us how to remove the word *can't* from our vocabulary, and that was what I did. I took a public-speaking class and an English class, and I passed the two semesters with a B- in each class. I was now beginning to build up my confidence.

This time, I was attentive in class and punctual, and most of all, I respected my instructors. There wasn't any more time for me to act out, no more room for immature behavior. I began feeling good about myself. I attended college at night, and during the day, I had opened up my own small body shop called Skip's Collision. I rented a stall from Ken and Ray (at D&W). I repaired all makes and models, but my specialty was Corvette repair. Everyone knew me for my perfection, and I liked the positive reinforcement I received when customers picked up their cars after I repaired them.

Christine

I had been dating off and on after returning home from my six months of active duty in the army, but I wanted a relationship that would fulfill my emotional needs. In late September, my close friend Joe and I were walking back to our cars after our college classes ended, and I ran into to this chick I had met at a New Year's Eve party. Her name was Christine. In those days, I was still a bit apprehensive of who I dated and little bit on the shy side. (Me, shy? Hard to believe!) I said to Chris in a cool voice, "Hey, how ya doing?"

She, in return, said, "Hello."

My heart was pounding as I thought about asking her to go out with me. We all know the drill. No one wants to be rejected or get a NO for an answer. We exchanged some small talk. "What have you been up to?" and "How have you been?"

The conversation was going smooth, and I was thinking, "Should I ask her for her number or be cool and move on?" I said, "Catch you later." I maintained my coolness. Guys had to be smooth and cool. That was the thing to do.

I strutted out the door in a cool style and said to my good friend Joe, "Should I ask her for her phone number?"

He said, "Yeah, you better."

I turned around, went back inside, and said, "Chris, can I have your number?"

She said, "Yes."

I couldn't wait until I got home. I gave her a call and asked her out on a date—and again, she said yes. Before I picked Chris up for our date, I washed and waxed my dusty

1969 Pontiac GTO for the big evening. I couldn't take her out in a car that was not spotless. I wanted to make a good impression. I drove up to her home and parked my GTO in the street in front of her house. I walked up the drive knocked on the front door, and waited for someone to answer. Chris opened the door and said, "Hi, come on in. I want you to meet my parents. Mom and Dad," she said, "I want you to meet Frank."

I used my best manners and said, "It's nice to meet you." I shook her father's hand and acknowledged her mother. That was how we did it in those days. We always walked up to the door. We never laid on the horn and waited for the girl to jump in the car. If we did, we would get a scolding from the girl's father. We went to a movie and afterwards, we talked endlessly that night, sharing our likes and dislikes. We hit it off immediately.

Two weeks later, I proposed to her. I knew she was the one for me. I was nineteen when I proposed to Chris, who was 371 days younger than me. (God forbid if I were to disclose her age. Heaven help me!) Now I knew I had to dig in and get serious regarding my future and finances. I needed a steady income and job security. I needed to save money and pay off my debts before we made that lifelong commitment to each other.

I set my goals high, as we were about to embark on a journey of spending our lives together—forever! Chris was and will always be my soul mate. Our relationship of forty-six years of marriage continues to be strong. Chris and I were married one and a half years after I proposed, on April 23, 1971.

Becoming a Man

Preparing for the Wedding

1970–1971

I needed job security, and I needed it fast. I knew the days of Skip's Collision were coming to an end. The money that I was making was irregular and inconsistent. I needed stability in my life if I wanted to fulfill my promises to Chris.

Everything was going through my head. Being married meant I would have additional financial responsibilities—health insurance, grocery money—and I would soon be the person responsible for paying all of the bills. No more would I be spending all of my money on a cool car. My new priorities would be to support our household expenses and my new wife.

Working in a productive collision shop just wasn't happening. I was twenty years old and still hadn't found that dream job where I could use my years of experience. Interview after interview, I had no luck. It was like a recording: "We will get back to you." And they never did.

In the late 1960s and early 1970s, you had to know someone to get into a collision shop or a dealership. My soon-to-be wife said, "My uncle Bill can get you a job at Ford Motor Company." As much as I didn't want it, I swallowed my pride and accepted the position from Uncle Bill. I was hired in at the Ford axle plant, and was soon working on the assembly line.

Ford Assembly Plant, Livonia
By Dwight Burdette (Own work) [CC BY 3.0
(http://creativecommons.org/licenses/by/3.0)]

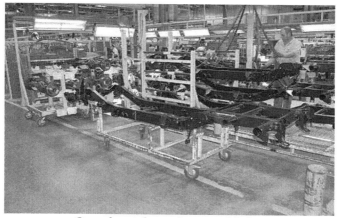

One of my jobs on the assembly line
By Bahnfrend (Own work) [CC BY-SA 3.0
(https://creativecommons.org/licenses/by-sa/3.0)]

I reported to work on the same day that I filled out my application. I was to work on the midnight shift, 10:00 p.m. to 6:30 a.m. My work was very repetitive—every day, it was the same thing. The line stopped for no one. As one shift left, the other shift began. Over and over, the production line kept going. Over and over and over . . . .

Everyone had given me the same old advice: "You should go to work in the factory. You will make good money and receive excellent health benefits in case you and your wife decide to have a baby."

Work on the assembly line in an automotive plant bored me. I knew I couldn't have it my way all the time, so I punched in and out of work every night, over and over and over. I worked at the Ford Motor Company's Sterling Heights factory. I hated my job, and knew I could offer the world so much more than simply being a human robot. But was the stability, a regular paycheck, and benefits worth it? I was miserable.

My job did change every now and then. One week, I would be lifting axle shafts and placing them on an automated machine to have axle bearings installed. The next three weeks, I would be at the end of the assembly line removing the axle assemblies and preparing them to be shipped nationwide. I was moved from workstation to workstation within the plant. I had some hope of possibly advancing to a more dignified, challenging position one day. I never refused to do anything I was asked to do. I wanted to be a good employee. I said to myself as I showed my ID badge, "Welcome to the Rock. Don't even think of quitting. You will be here for the next thirty years." I felt that I was reporting for a prison sentence, and wanted to yell, "Hey, I am innocent!"

It was now January of 1971 and the beginning of a new year. I had a lot going on. Chris and I would be getting married in April, our new home was almost ready to move into, and I was working day and night to pay for everything that would be coming due soon. Chris already had a well-paying job and a career going for herself at the United States Steel Corporation. Together, we were on a mission to succeed as a couple.

On a minus-two-degree winter evening, I drove my car in the Michigan winter, and the roads were slippery, snow-covered from a storm earlier in the morning. Yet, all the schools were closed, and the weatherman was saying, "Please stay off the roads." The factories were open. They rarely closed down for anything, including the weather. The motto was "The assembly line stops for no one! Production must continue!" So I sucked it up and I drove on the treacherous roads and reported to my job on the assembly line. I punched in and walked to my assigned workstation, my foreman, Keith, walked up to me and said, "Frank, we are going to move you to spindle lathe."

I said, "Spindle lathe?"

We walked over to the lathe, and the guy who was to train me showed me how it worked. He also showed me all of his scars from the spindles that flew out of the machine at a high speed. He said, "See this scar? And how about this one? Frank, you have to be careful. You could lose your eye or a finger." The goal of production per night was 1,250 pieces.

I said to myself, "Are you shitting me? I am not losing any of my body parts for this job." Yet, I started working on it, but my production rate was a thousand less than the former operator; it dropped to about 225 to 260 parts per eight-hour shift. My foreman came up to me and said, "Frank, what's the problem?"

I raised my two hands and said, "These two hands know how to do bodywork, and I am not going to lose them for this job."

He said, "What the hell are you working on an assembly line for?"

I told him my age was working against me, and I was getting married in April, and I needed this job and the money.

He said, "Kid, don't waste your life in here. Find a job in the body shop. Go out and make big money. Do the best you can do."

The next day, I went over to Chris's mom and dad's house and looked in the local newspaper. I saw an ad that read, "Wanted: Auto-Body Man. Must have own tools. Must be sober and dependable. Call for appointment." It was 4:40 p.m. when I nervously called to make an appointment for an interview. The man who answered the phone said, "If you are interested in the job, get your ass down here before 5:00 p.m. I'm not waiting for you."

I asked, "Where are you located?"

He said, "Twelve and a Half Mile Road and Woodward."

I said, "I'll be right there!"

It was a typical Michigan winter day, the traffic was heavy, the roads were slippery and I had only twenty minutes to drive approximately fifteen miles. I drove as carefully as I could, but I didn't stop for any yellow lights. I arrived five minutes before 5 o'clock.

I went right into the office and introduced myself. He was a big man, with a brush-cut hairstyle and saliva running down the cigar he had in his mouth. He was wearing a gray sports coat that had seen better days and a stained tight-fitting turtleneck shirt. He was very intimidating as he towered over me. I couldn't let him see that I was nervous and badly wanted this job and the opportunity to start back doing what I'd always dreamed of doing.

I put out my right hand, and with a firm handshake, I said, "My name is Frank Antonucci. Thank you for giving me this opportunity to be interviewed."

I did not show him that I was intimidated by his size. He said, "Sit down." He began to ask me a series of questions. "OK, kid. You look awful young to be working in the body shop. What do you know at your age? How much experience do you have? Do you know how to do lead and metal finishing?"

In my days working with Frank Mini at R&M Collision, he had taught me how to do lead and metal finishing. Frank was the best in the business. Everyone knew who Frank Mini is and said how good of a metal-finisher and lead man he was. I thought, I learned from the best, and I knew what I was doing. I was confident about answering the question. Mr. Intimidator would not rock my confidence. I said I could do the two processes he was asking me.

He said, "Do you have a f–ing toolbox and tools?"

I said, "Yes."

He said, "Get your f–ing ass here in the morning at seven thirty. Do I make myself clear?"

I said, "Yes, sir!"

Then he went on to say, "I got to get the f—k out of here. The roads are bad."

The next morning, I would be working for the Wilson Crissman Cadillac dealership as a body man on 50 percent commission. I left the interview at 6:30 p.m. and had to report to the Ford factory to work the midnight shift.

I reported to my Ford foreman, Keith, gave him my notice and turned in my badge. That night was my last night working on that assembly line. As I exited through the turnstile gates, I felt my prison sentence had been commuted. I hoped I would never have to work on an assembly line again.

My New Job at the Dealership

I had finally made the big time. I was working at a prestigious Cadillac dealer located in Oakland County. My pay was 50 percent commission of the labor. The more cars I repaired, the more money I made. There were four body men and two painters. I was the new kid in the shop, and therefore, I received the fewest cars. I still made a decent amount of money.

However, Dick, the manager, appeared to have it out for me, and I didn't know why. He knew I needed the money, and I was only a few weeks away from getting married to Chris. Once again, I had put myself in a position that I couldn't control. I needed this job, and I needed to build a good reputation. To be hired at the age of twenty-one in a body shop was a difficult thing to do. Dick would harass me daily, and I didn't know why. My metal-finishing and lead work were spot on, and all the guys in the shop knew it. They would say, "Nice job! That really came out good." Dick couldn't find anything wrong in the bodywork I did or the cars that were repaired in my stall. I arrived at work before my scheduled workday began. I had all of my own tools, and I repaired every damaged car he put in my stall. I could not figure out what his problem with me was. However, he would regularly bust my balls for no reason. The guys told me not to worry about him and clued me in that he was a number-one prick and not respected by any of his crew.

One of the painters whom I befriended was Bob, and he knew how to paint. His work was flawless. He was my age, and we worked well together. Chris continued working for United States Steel Corporation. The money she brought in was a plus.

Then our big day was here. I took a week off (unpaid), and Chris and I went on our honeymoon. We had purchased a new home, and we were off to a good beginning.

When I returned to the shop, everyone appeared to be glad to see me except Dick. I think he couldn't wait to bust my balls again. It was now April of 1971, and spring was in the air. The busy season for the body-shop business in Michigan was during the winter months. Those icy, snow-covered roads could be treacherous to drive on since they created hazardous driving conditions and therefore, many collisions. In the spring and summer months, the collision business always slowed down.

We were all on commission, and our paystubs reflected the good season and the slow season. Bob and I began doing side work to make extra money, and we actually made more money on the side than we made at our full-time jobs. We did this very quietly because we didn't want the tyrant Dick to find out. Two or three weeks after I returned from my honeymoon, Dick called me into the office. I will never forget his words.

"I have to fire you."

I was in shock. I asked, "Why?"

He said that my work was terrible, and I couldn't keep up with the workload.

I said, "I never had any complaints from the painters and never had any jobs that I had to redo."

He said, "It doesn't matter. Get the f—k out of here."

I was devastated and embarrassed. I had never been fired. I left his office, and the senior painter (Harold), who had been there long before Dick, said, "Kid, don't worry about him. Leave your toolbox there and go home."

I said, "F—k this place. I am leaving!"

He said again, "Kid, listen to me," but I couldn't. My pride was crushed. Later on in the afternoon, I packed up my tools, hung my head low, and vacated the premises in shame. Bob, my soon-to-be business partner, quit the same day.

The next morning, Harold called me and said, "They fired Dick for firing you." I felt vindicated, but didn't go back; Bob and I had made a master plan: a collision shop of our own.

National Body Repair

1971–1975

Bob and I began to do referral work in a one-and-a-half-car garage located in Hazel Park, Michigan. That one-and-a-half-car garage reminded me of my days living on Erben Street. It meant we could only do one car at a time. Our reputation was excellent and we were known for our quality, so our clientele grew. As our customers picked up their repaired vehicles, repeatedly they said to us, "Wow! I can't even tell where the repair work was done."

Soon, the word spread, and we were doing two and three cars at a time. I was fortunate that Chris kept her job at United States Steel Corporation. This provided us with a regular income. Working out of a small garage was great as long as the Michigan weather was nice and sunny. On rainy days, we were at a standstill. Soon the fall and winter seasons would close in on us. Our customer referrals began to grow, and we needed to get serious and get more space if we were to succeed in business.

Bob and I were both twenty-one years old and confident in our areas of expertise. Bob was the painter, and I was the body man. We were a great combination. Yet, we discovered that simply being proficient in our specialty areas wasn't sufficient to sustain a business and we needed to expand.

Experienced business owners tried to explain the many aspects of being in business. However, at twenty-one years old, we were also a bit arrogant. No one could tell us anything. After all, we thought we knew what we were doing – on a mission to make a name for ourselves. We thought seriously about opening up a body shop and going big time to make lots of money. The American dream seemed within our grasp.

We searched for a building and a location. We didn't have any experience or the necessary finances to do so. Our partnership was supposed to be fifty-fifty, or so I thought. As it turned out, Bob's financial contribution was $1,000 and mine was $10,000, thanks to the generosity of my father-in-law. He loaned me the money to get started. He truly believed in me and was a great man.

So, right from the beginning, we were off to a start that was not fifty-fifty, and later on, that would be our downfall and demise. I didn't see it at the time. We found a location in an industrial complex located off of a major road in Fraser, Michigan.

The building was four thousand square feet, and when it was empty, it looked as big as a football stadium. Bob and I contacted a lawyer to do the necessary paper work, and then we opened up a shop. We called our business National Body Repair. We plunged ahead and didn't ask any experienced business owners their advice. They recommended to us that we open our business as an LLC, not a DBA.[12] We thought that having a business name was enough.

I trusted everyone, and as I said before, I thought I knew everything. We met the location and zoning requirements, and we were off and running. Now, instead of our previous one-and-a-half-car garage with one car inside, we had a building large enough to hold fourteen cars. When there was only one car inside our new building, it was scary. Our rent was $650 per month.

Bob and I didn't have a clue what being a business owner and running a body shop actually entailed. We never thought about the rest of our commitments and overhead expenses such as (just to name a few) gas, electric, taxes, insurance, and supplies. And oh, I almost forgot, our salaries.

It *was* really nice to say, "I co-own National Body Repair" and be cool to impress everyone. I didn't enjoy doing the paper work for the business, so we divided up our responsibilities. Bob handled the banking, taxes, bookkeeping, and payroll. My responsibilities included writing estimates, ordering parts, talking to insurance

---

[12] A limited liability company (LLC) is a corporate structure whereby the members of the company cannot be held personally liable for the company's debts or liabilities. Limited liability companies are essentially hybrid entities that combine the characteristics of a corporation and a partnership or sole proprietorship.

A DBA is different. Sometimes it makes sense for a company to do business under a different name. To do this, the company has to file what's known as a DBA—an abbreviation for "doing business as." A DBA is also known as a fictitious business name, a trade name, or an assumed name.

companies, acquiring new accounts, and managing the shop area.

We had done so well in the small garage in Hazel Park, we thought we could do all of the above and repair the vehicles as if we had supernatural powers. We had our wives and family life to take care of also.

As our business began to grow, we realized we couldn't do all the repairs ourselves and run a business effectively. The workload became backlogged, and the customers wanted their cars back. So we hired our first employee, thinking this would be the answer for our shop. We didn't know how much to pay him and didn't take into consideration the increase in our overhead expenses. The reality of owning a business was beginning to sink in, but we were committed and couldn't turn back.

We had never made out a payroll check for an employee, so contacted a Certified Public Accountant. We also needed to know how and what to do with federal and state taxes. Oh, how I wished I had paid more attention in my business math classes. I couldn't believe all of the taxes a business owner had to pay over and above the cost of operating a business. For example, we didn't know we had to pay the government matching funds for FICA[13]—another expense we never counted on. Being in business wasn't as easy as we had thought.

When we were working in a one-car garage, there was no overhead, rent, gas, electric, water or taxes. A car would be dropped off for repair. We charged $100. We took out $25

---

[13] Federal Insurance Contributions Act (FICA) tax is a United States federal payroll (or employment) tax imposed on both employees and employers to fund Social Security and Medicare.

for supplies, and then we split our profit. That was $37.50 each, which was not bad. Now we did the same repair at the shop, and the profit of $75 was deposited in the shop's bank account to pay the bills. First of all, the rent was $650. And there were additional bills due every month without fail. This never figured into our business plan because we didn't know what a business plan was. We hadn't listened to anyone.

We soon began to realize we needed to bring in more cars and money. As the volume of work grew, our need for more employees also increased. In our first full year of being in business, we grossed over $105,000, and that was outstanding in the early 1970s. However, our net was less than 10 percent of that number ($10,500), which was not impressive.

We couldn't manage our money—it was that simple. Although we were the busiest shop around, we barely made enough money to keep us in the black. We were busy because our quality of work was second to none. However, the prices we charged were so low, we couldn't make a profit. We didn't get it. We thought if we raised our prices, we would lose our clientele.

Our own paychecks were sporadic at best. The business continued to grow, and we had more and more customers who wanted National Body Repair to repaint and rebuild their pride and joys—their cars. In 1973, we expanded from four thousand square feet to twelve thousand square feet, and we had twelve employees. The bigger we grew, the smaller our profits were, and the more we had to pay everyone except ourselves.

We were making daily bank deposits, but in reality, we were robbing Peter to pay Paul. We were exchanging dollars, not making dollars. The money would come in and go out just as fast. We continued to pay everyone except the two big shots who owned the business. Not getting paid began to wear on us and our families. I kept thinking I couldn't disappoint my father-in-law and lose his investment.

I remembered that Bob had only risked $1,000 to my $10,000. He had little to lose if we folded. Bob's attitude began to change, and I could see the writing on the wall. Bob felt defeated, and he was giving up. We were getting burned out from all of our hard work for our efforts. It was disheartening not being able to enjoy the benefits of being business owners we'd dreamed of. I finally thought about everything that others had tried to tell us. Maybe all those people who had tried to talk to and coach me weren't wrong after all.

By 1974, tension grew between Bob and me, and being in business together was no longer attractive. The end was in sight, but I didn't know how or when a split would happen. We both had financial commitments and contracts to fulfill, but for me, the most important thing was paying back the $10,000 my father-in-law had loaned me. What was I going to do, and how would I repay him? I realized our partnership was not a true fifty-fifty split. I had been warned over and over to watch my back, but no, I was Mr. Nice Guy and wouldn't listen to anyone.

Bob and I finally decided to part ways, and he suggested I buy him out. How could I buy him out when we owed so much? The deal I gave him was ridiculously in his favor, and that haunted me for years to come. Again, I should have listened to the advice I was offered.

Bob and I had been good friends, so I viewed our split as personal, not as a business transaction. I didn't want bad feelings between the two of us. So I let Bob walk away from the business debt-free. In our case, I was the one responsible for all remaining debts. What was I thinking? Who was I listening to? NO ONE! One of my employees had told me, "The rate of the surviving partner succeeding with a business after a split is less than 25 percent."

I said to myself, "Thanks for the vote of confidence!"

In the beginning, I thought, "This will be easy. I can do this." That is, until I began to reorganize the office. I found my worst nightmare: the quarterly Internal Revenue payment schedule. Although we had withheld the payroll taxes, Bob had never sent in the quarterly returns to the feds or the State of Michigan. I was furious and came unglued. How could I have let this happen? How could I have been so irresponsible? I further discovered various bills that had been past due for over a month. I found a letter from the phone company that read, "Failure to pay by the named date means service will be interrupted."

I thought, "Holy shit." Without the phone, we couldn't communicate. Without the electricity, we couldn't operate. What was I to do now? Soon after that, an Internal Revenue Agent showed up.

The shop was filled to capacity. I had twelve employees, and owed everyone money. And I had to repay my father-in-law. Chris had quit her job in mid-1972 as she waited for our first child to be born, so we didn't have her salary. I was in deep trouble and couldn't see daylight at the end of the tunnel. The pressure was growing, and I had to come up with a plan to turn this around. Yet, I kept thinking, "I can do it and beat the odds."

I soon learned that being a business owner meant also being a bookkeeper, custodian, loan and finance officer, babysitter, and good articulator with the customers. My first priority should have been my family—being a husband and soon-to-be father. But I was so far in debt that my only focus was the shop. I began to forget who I was, and I failed to recognize who I was becoming.

Chris tolerated my long hours away from home for a reasonable amount of time. However, as our baby neared delivery, her patience began wearing thin. On January 16, 1973, we were blessed with our first son. I cried with joy when Dr. Dutcher said to me, "Your wife delivered a healthy baby boy!" There was an adjustment period for Chris and me as we welcomed little Frankie into our family.

I looked for ways to cut the overhead down at the shop to make it profitable. I kept reminding myself that I knew how to paint and do the bodywork. And I told myself that I could turn this business around.

There was one thing I didn't have, and that was a business attitude. I was very gullible too. My customers would give me a sad story as they came in to pick up their cars. My body shop was responsible for collecting the insurance deductibles and monies owed for any additional work the customer requested. But when I heard excuses, I bought their stories hook, line, and sinker . . . *I forgot my checkbook." "I don't get paid until Friday." "The insurance paid you enough, and I shouldn't have to pay my deductible." "The accident wasn't my fault." "The insurance company said they waived my deducible."*

126

It was simple—I wasn't a good businessman. I should have simply said, "I understand. I will place your vehicle in storage, and when the funds are available, pay me and I will give you your vehicle. I will not charge you any storage fees for the first three days. Have a good day." End of discussion. If I were the type of person who could say this to my customers, I would have had a decent chance of survival.

I decided to relocate, against the advice of my current landlord. He was trying to help me and work with me, but I panicked, and once again I didn't listen to someone experienced, which was another huge mistake.

I was now twenty-four years old and in debt up to my neck. I still owed my father in-law $10,000. I was stressed out, and that says it all. I began exploring my options, and downsizing seemed to be my only way out of this mess. The current size of the shop was 12,000 sq. and the size of my new location was 4,500 sq. I believed a move would turn the shop around and make it profitable again.

However more lessons were to be learned. I never considered the age of the building, furnace, ingress and egress, age of the roof, the many glass windows, city restrictions, and building codes and moving costs.

Chris was expecting our second child, and her pregnancy was difficult. The strain on our family was increasing, and our future together didn't seem too bright. Tension was in the air, and I began to realize I couldn't turn things around.

On January 1, 1975, Chris had a baby girl. We named her Christina, and now we were a family of four. Then an ultimatum came down from Chris. She said, "The business goes, or I go."

A few months after our daughter's birth, we received a pamphlet in the mail from Warren Consolidated Schools announcing that they had received approval to build a school centered on skilled trades. One of the classes being taught there would be auto-body repair. Chris showed me the pamphlet, and I said, "That's nice." I didn't think much more about it.

Then, one of my customers said as he dropped off his Corvette, "You would make a good teacher."

I said, "Really?"

He said, "Yes, you have what it takes to become a good teacher."

I started to think about it and discussed this with Chris. She gave me some much-needed confidence and encouraged me to apply for the position. She said, "Honey, you can do this, and the students will love you. You're a natural." She supported me 100 percent.

I thought back to my high-school days and all the BS stories I had used to escape accountability. I thought being a good body man would be sufficient. How wrong I was! I contacted Warren Consolidated Schools to learn more about the position as auto-body teacher at the soon-to-be-built school. The human-resources person said to come over, pick up the application, fill it out, and be sure to attach my résumé.

I said politely, "Thank you!" and left. I started to think about my résumé, and I realized I didn't have a clue how to properly prepare a résumé. The day we covered résumés in English class, I must have been dreaming of being in an auto shop. "Who needs a résumé anyway? I don't."

I asked my brother in-law Tom to help me write my résumé and he patiently worked with me step by step. With Tom's help I completed and submitted my first resume ever. I sent my application and my newly crafted résumé to the WCS human sources department. They contacted me, I had several interviews, and in July 1975, I received a phone call from human resources. "This is Dr. Jim from human resources, and we would like to offer you a contract."

I was in shock. Chris had been right all along. I could do this! I promised myself I would become a good teacher. Just eight short years had passed since my graduation from Lakeview High School. The past eight years of my work life had been wild and unfulfilling. I couldn't wait to begin something new in September of that same year.

It was July of 1975 and I still owned National Body Repair at our new location in Roseville, Michigan. I still struggled to keep it going. I contacted a lawyer, and he told me to bring my all my account books and records to him so we could discuss the future of the business. We met and talked about an hour, and he said he would get back to me after reviewing my records. A few days later, he told me, "I recommend that you declare bankruptcy immediately."

I asked, "Why are you recommending bankruptcy?"

He said, "You're too far in debt to turn it around. You owe a huge amount of money to the State of Michigan and the federal government. You don't have a chance."

For the first time, I finally decided to listen to someone who was giving me good advice. I said, "What do I do? What do I say?"

He said, "Notify your employees, have them remove their personal belongings, and lock the door behind you.

Bring me the keys. You will be finished and no longer in business."

So, in late October 1975, National Body Repair went out of business. I kept hearing those old familiar voices inside my head saying to me, "What will people say? What will people think? I am a failure." That was only the stubborn and proud Italian coming out of me. I owed the Federal Government and the State of Michigan over $65,000 and could not pay it.

I discussed repayment for the $10,000 with my father-in law. It took me years to repay him, but I finally did. I paid him back. He always trusted and believed in me. My father-in-law was OK with my decision to close the shop and proud that I was beginning a new career as a teacher. He also knew there was a lot of stress in our household, but he didn't know how much. Chris and I didn't take our family issues outside of our home. As I look back on the business episode of my life, let's say I am glad it's over.

Thank you to my father-in-law, Joseph A. Guadagnino.

Back to School

The New Teacher

It was 1975, and *Saturday Night Fever* and the new disco craze were going on. The Bee Gees were singing "Staying Alive," and Donna Summer was singing "Hot Stuff." Polyester and platform shoes were in style.

A Couple of Cool Cats

Chris had gone shopping and bought me some new school clothes. I walked in the door from work at the shop one day, and Chris said, "Hi, honey. I went shopping for you today at Hudson's Department Store." She showed me the three polyester suits she had purchased for me: one dark brown, one powder blue, and one kelly green. She had also bought a pair of brown platform shoes. "Try everything on," she said.

"OK." Everything fit just fine. I could see a glow of happiness in her eyes. I knew she always wanted the best for me and the kids. I felt blessed that she stood by me through all the ups and downs since we had known each other.

I couldn't sleep the night before I began my new job as a teacher—and an auto-body teacher at that! I had set the alarm for 6:00 a.m. My start time was at 7:00 a.m. and we lived less than a mile from the school. Chris and I got up quietly because we didn't want to wake Frankie and Christina.

Chris made the coffee as I got dressed. For the first time in our married life, I was reporting to a job that the good Lord had provided for me! We were both excited. As I walked into the kitchen, I was greeted with a kiss from my loving wife. She complimented me on how nice and professional I looked. I was nervous and still lacked self-confidence. After all, I was going to work as a high-school auto body teacher and classroom teaching was a brand new experience for me. My classroom assignment was to teach students fifteen- to eighteen-years-old how to do the fine art of auto-body repair. I reported to work for my first staff meeting for a teacher orientation day. This staff meeting was held two days before the students' first day of school.

Here I was, sitting among my soon-to-be peers, thinking, "Me, a teacher?" As I sat, patiently waiting for the meeting to begin, I listened to everyone talking about their summer vacations and the trips they had been on with their families. My stomach began turning. I was excited and nauseated at the same.

This was a brand new stand-alone school that had been approved by the State of Michigan and the Warren Consolidated School District. This project was state, local, and federally funded. The man who had the vision and who convinced the district to build the school was the current vocational director. His name was Alfred Braciano, and he wanted us to call him Al. The name of this new school was the Career Preparation Center or CPC for short.

The teacher sitting next to me leaned over and said, "We have eleven weeks until our Thanksgiving break."

I thought, "Why would he say that?"

I introduced myself to him. His name was Bob, and little did I know that this fellow teacher would become the man who would mentor and guide me thorough the many challenges I was about to encounter. In the beginning, I felt intimidated and inferior. I kept thinking, "I was in the C group in school. How could I ever become a schoolteacher?"

Soon the principal and the vocational director, Al Braciano, walked into the room, and our first staff meeting began. We were welcomed, introduced and given instructions about what we needed to do to get the new school year started. At first it was overwhelming. I had to become familiar with all the acronyms. In education, the jargon can be overwhelming if you're not familiar with it.

I started to meet and talk to my colleagues and discovered I was not the only person without a teaching certificate. I was hired for my knowledge and experience and not because I held a teaching degree. One of the conditions of my being hired was that I would pursue a teaching degree in order to retain my position. I thought, "Teaching degree. Who, me?"

That was why it was so important to enroll in college. I knew how to do auto-body repair, but I had no clue how to be a classroom teacher. Al asked me to join him for lunch after the staff meeting. He said, "How are you doing?"

I said, "I thank you and God that I was hired for this position."

Al went on to say in a Don Corleone–style voice, "Young man, you will go to college, and you will get a teaching certificate. Do you understand me?"

I smiled and said, "Yes, sir! I will enroll in college as soon as I can. I will not disappoint you and this school district."

The construction workers were putting the finishing touches on the building and my room was in organized chaos, boxes were everywhere waiting to be opened and inventoried. As I entered my new classroom, all of the equipment and textbooks were in a pile on the floor in the center of the shop. I didn't have a traditional classroom. Therefore, I was placed wherever they could find space for me.

The students' first day of school was the day after Labor Day, 1975. Over the Labor Day weekend, we had our traditional family barbeque. As the day came to an end everyone said their good-byes and wished me well on my first day of the job. I was excited to go on a new journey in my life. The very next day, I would meet my first auto shop students.

Thank you, Al Braciano.

Meeting the Class

Each teacher had a mailbox in the main office. During our previous staff orientation meeting, we were advised to check our mailboxes daily, prior to the beginning of class. The boxes were in alphabetical order by our names, and mine was first on the top left row. I reached in, and there it was: my class list, which contained the names of all of the new students who were assigned to my program. There were a total of fifty-five, all boys. We were in the 1970s, and girls didn't enroll in a shop class. That wasn't a trendy option in those days.

As I walked down the hallway, I saw a group of guys standing outside the classroom door, leaning against the walls. They appeared to be bored out of their minds. I walked inside the classroom, and I saw a few kids sitting there. I said good morning to them. I heard the bell ring and the guys who had been standing in the hall entered my classroom. The room was small. I could feel all eyes staring me down. I wasn't sure whether they were staring at my leisure suit or me.

I proceeded to take roll call and connect names with faces. I said to myself, "Holy crap, what have I gotten myself into?" I knew I had to connect with them fast, or I would lose the continuity of the program and their respect.

I had graduated from high school in 1967. This was 1975—eight year's difference. "Make connections NOW!" I thought. I proceeded to share my knowledge and background. I had to come down to their level so they could come up to mine. I made their first day of class interesting enough that they wanted to return the next day. I was open and honest with my students and told them that we had a lot of work to do to prepare our new classroom for move-in.

The classroom—it was commonly known as the "body shop"—would be the foundation of the program. These kids were mostly those who wanted to work with their hands and not sit behind a desk and become pencil pushers. Most of these kids were academic underachievers, much like myself, and did not participate in sports. They were often referred to as "those kids." I was upset to hear people refer to my students this way. I had once been one of "those kids."

I still found it sad that we are only measured by our academic success or how well we hit a baseball or throw a football. I believe team sports can be a good thing and build character. However, many of those who are the stars on their high-school teams have a void after their senior year of high school has ended. After they realize they won't be a star on a big college team and they are no longer in the limelight (as they had been their high school), they feel let a huge let down. After the pep rallies end and they haven't made it to the big leagues like they and their parents dreamed about, they have an empty feeling.

My students were a gift to me. I could teach them a skill and build up their confidence that would hopefully stay with them for the rest of their lives. I knew I had to develop teaching strategies that would allow me to reach students at all academic levels.

The classroom period was three hours long, and students would earn three credits. I thought, "How am I going to keep these tough guys interested in my program and maintain classroom control?" I knew I wanted the best for them. I wanted them to realize their success could be measured by acquiring skills.

Please do not misunderstand me when I refer to sports and academia. There are students who excel in those areas, and that's great. My students were those who had been repeatedly passed up because they just didn't fit in. They were gearheads. I connected with this because I lived it. I was now in a position where I was able to change the course of their destiny and give them a future to build on.

My group was diversified. They came from different backgrounds, and most of them expressed low self-esteem. So I needed to give them confidence as they learned their career skills. I also needed to build trust and establish student-teacher boundaries, so the communication lines could open up. I started out by helping them experience fun in the classroom. Once their fear of learning new skills left, the students would confide in me how discouraged they felt because some of their peers and teachers looked down upon them when they couldn't understand the academic subjects. They just wanted to fit in like everyone else. At times, I felt as if I were looking into a mirror as I reflected on my days being in the notorious C group.

The students soon shortened my name and dubbed me Mr. A. I liked that! It showed me they were feeling comfortable in our classroom.

Classroom Strategies

The first year of teaching was a growing experience for me. I will never forget what I learned. I had my first negative encounter with two students who were being disrespectful to me and the class. I said to them, "You're going to the office to get the paddle."

They laughed out loud and said, "We're not going to the office for the paddle."

I was lost for words. I called my buddy Bob and said, "Bob, I want to send these two guys down to office for the paddle."

The Paddle A.K.A. The Wood

Bob said, "Paddle? Where have you been? The paddle was outlawed, and we do not give the paddle in school. What's going on down there?"

"I have a couple of tough guys giving me a hard time."

He said, "Welcome to Education 101. You will need to take care of this on your own. Can you do it?" All through my life, I have been blessed with mentors, people who guided me through areas that I was new to. Bob was who the Lord put into my life. What a great guy to know.

I said, "Yeah, I can do it. I will not let these two punks bring me down and destroy my class."

I returned to the front of my class and said, "You guys are right. There is no more paddle. I apologize for saying that to you. Now pack up your personal belongings and get the hell out of my classroom and don't come back."

I knew that two of them were seniors. Without the three credits from my class, Bill and Dave would not graduate.

They said, "Please, Mr. A. We need the credits from this class to graduate."

I said to them in front of the class, "I see the two of you are wearing letterman's jackets. Are you still on the team?"

"Yes, we are on the football team."

I said, "Is this how you behave on the football field? Would your coach put up with this the type of behavior?"

"No, Mr. A."

"How old are you guys?"

"Seventeen and eighteen."

In a loud drill-sergeant voice, I said, "Then act like it! Do you understand me?"

"Yes, sir!"

"Take a seat and welcome back to my classroom."

That day, the tone of my classroom began to change. I was able to maintain everyone's attention. The more I demonstrated that I believed in them, the more they gravitated toward me. I began to respect my students, and they, in return, respected me as their teacher. I made it very clear I was not going to let anyone destroy the integrity of the program. I also realized that I could get my point across without the use of corporal punishment (the paddle).

The first year was rough, a learning experience for me as well as the students. I wanted to be fair and firm, and to have fun in my classroom. If I didn't develop an effective teaching style in my first year, it would be very difficult to correct it and turn it around in my second year.

My philosophy was simple. The classroom should be a place where it was fun to learn, where kids felt safe, and most of all, where the limitations and guidelines were clearly understood by the students. I was up front with my students. They always knew where I was coming from. I made it clear and I often said, "We are not here to play games. We are here to learn a skill."

Students (kids) are not that different from adults. We all want to be respected and trusted. My classroom was structured as if we were working in the real world. Through trial and error, I developed a specific set of guidelines. They were easy to follow for all of the students. I discovered out of the twenty-five students enrolled in each session, there were twenty-five different personalities and learning styles. I couldn't believe how many students who were in the eleventh and twelfth grades still struggled with basic academic issues. I had struggled in school, but I hadn't been as lost as some of these kids in my class. I wondered how they had made it to the eleventh or twelfth grade.

I wanted to know who my students were on a personal level—that would enable me to help them grow and develop—so I created an exercise. Wow, what an eye opener for me!

I said to them, "Take out a sheet of paper and a pencil."

I didn't expect to hear what they said next. They said, "What?"

I said, "Take out a piece of paper and a pencil."

For a moment, I wondered if I was speaking in a different language. Someone said to me, "I ain't here to use a paper and pencil. I am here to work on cars."

I now knew the true meaning of coming to class prepared. I began at step one—giving everyone the material they needed to work with: that is, a piece of paper and a pencil. I shared with the class who I was and why I wanted to become their teacher. I wanted them to feel wanted and know who I was.

So I said to them, "I want to know who you are. Therefore, I want you to write down the following questions and answer them."

I could hear more mumbling. "Why do we have to do this junk?" someone asked.

I said, "Just do it!"

The five questions were these:

How many brothers and sisters do you have?

What's your relationship with your parents like?

Do you work after school?

Do you have duties and responsibilities around the house?

What is your reason for taking the class, and what do you expect to get out of it?

I collected the papers and asked them to return the pencils to me. This in-class assignment was given to them on a Friday. I took the papers home and read and re-read them. I couldn't believe what I was reading? The papers looked as if they were written in hieroglyphics. I asked my wife to read them, and she was amazed at the variations in spelling.

She asked me, "What grade level are you teaching?"

I said, "Eleventh and twelfth grades." She just shook her head.

I was able to read through their errors and absorb the information, learning who my students were and where they were in their lives, including their family backgrounds and birth order. Reading their responses was truly a blessing. I was on a mission to change the culture of these kids. I wanted to be an effective teacher and maintain integrity in my classroom.

Their information allowed me to develop individual lesson plans for each of my students to help them learn the lessons being taught. I discovered they had many different learning styles. I had students who could not read and write very well but who were outstanding with their hands-on skills. I also had those who were proficient at reading and writing but fell short with hands-on skills. And finally, there were those students who had given up and were not confident about doing or trying anything new and exciting. They had become complacent about just getting by in school.

However, I will ask you, the reader a question: Can you identify with my students? This may be a rhetorical question, but deep down inside, I know what your answer will be. We are all different, some learn best one way, others another way.

I designed my tests to be fair. I tried to give each student the opportunity to excel. I began to develop lessons for all their different learning styles. I wanted to build up their confidence and give them some bragging rights.

There were two components built into my tests. One was based on theory, and the other was based on their hands-on training. However, to comply with state and local regulations, I had to have written documentation to support the hands-on portion of my lessons.

My written tests were in a basic language that the students could understand. They were designed so each of them had every opportunity to pass. Yet they were accountable to learn each lesson that I was teaching.

The hands-on tests were very rigid and tough. They either knew the process, or they didn't. There were no excuses. This type of testing gave them a chance to demonstrate their hands-on skills. In the real world, when you applied for a job in a body shop, the employer would want to see what you could do. After you were hired, you had to perform on the job. If you didn't, you were immediately fired. No questions asked. That was the way it was in a hands-on job; I'd learned that from my own experience.

As the students took their hands-on tests, I observed them to make sure they were correctly performing each of the specific lessons they were taught during the previous nine weeks in the auto-body shop. I would not accept any excuses from them. They either knew how to do something or they did not. Their future depended on it.

I knew my students well enough to know whether they were giving it 100 percent or trying to skate by. For those who gave it 100 percent, I continued to increase the challenge of the lessons, giving them a reason to grow and develop. I knew the ones who were there simply for the three credits and came down on them extra hard. I created several ways of motivating them, and some I won't mention here.

My rationale was to make them believe in themselves and give them hope and the sweet taste of success. There is a place for everyone who has a good attitude, a good work ethic, and a willingness to learn. I stressed this over and over and also reinforced that they would need to improve and grow within their academic areas as well.

In the real world, academic knowledge is used to complement hands-on skills. For example, I continuously reminded my student they needed to know their math skills to be able to mix paint formulas and regulate air viscosity coming out of the spray gun. Their pay rate would be based on a percentage of the dollar amount of work that was completed and turned in to the manager at the end of the workweek on Fridays. They didn't like their math classes and would often say to me "Were not here to do reading, writing and math Mr. A.". My classroom lessons and environment mimicked the appearance of a real life collision shop. First the students were required to (Write) an estimate on the vehicle that was to be repaired. Second the students were required to (Read) the part's manual and (Write) down the necessary parts required to repair the vehicle. Third and final part of the estimate is to total (Math) the amount of the parts and labor for the owner of the vehicle to approve. At the end of the class period on Fridays the students had to submit (Read-Write-Math) their simulated time cards. These time cards maintained the amount (Math) of hours they spent working on each vehicle. The written hours of work would then be converted (Math) to a dollar amount. This would simulate the amount of money earned for that week. They were beginning to have a clear understanding and the importance of paying attention to the academic part of high-school.

The auto-body program was a true hands-on program, and I presented many of my lessons in simple, hands-on and visual ways to help my students learn.

I'd gone through high school by lying low, not asking any questions, not causing trouble, just doing the minimum amount of work required to pass a class, and move on. I didn't want any of my students to go through my program and not learn a thing. These young, impressionable kids were my responsibility, and I would not let them slip through without learning. I was their teacher and the adult who was in control. I often reminded them that I was not there for a personality contest. I was there to teach them how to survive in the real world.

I also said to them, "You guys think I am tough. You will meet and work for people who will make me look like Peter Pan." Some days I had to discipline them and reinforce the classroom structure - how to behave like young adults - not like a group of babies. Doing this was all part of being a good teacher and mentor to each and every one of them.

At the end of each class period, we'd say our good-byes, and I told them that I looked forward to seeing them the next day. I was there to be their teacher. I never wanted them to say later that I didn't care about them and had passed them just to get rid of them. I wanted all of my students to like and respect me, but I knew deep down inside this was a fantasy, not reality. The truth hurts sometimes.

After my first year of teaching, I re-structured my grading system for the students, so they could all be successful. I wanted my students to understand my strict classroom limitations and their boundaries from Day One. I'd learned that maintaining classroom control at all times was first and foremost. If I didn't properly structure my classroom environment and put consequences into place, I'd have an uphill battle and likely would lose everything, including respect from the students.

I knew that if students didn't respect their teacher, they would not respect the lesson being taught. That would be the beginning of the end for me as their teacher. If the students went home and told their parents that our class was chaotic or out-of-control, the parents could call the principal, who would come down on me. The main office does not want to receive any phone calls from the parents regarding a teacher's performance.

As I look back at my first year of teaching, I realized the grace of God got me through it. My grading system was not the best. Yes, I knew how to do the hands-on part, but didn't know how to manage and control a structured classroom environment.

I was only eight years older than my students. I was naive and had never thought of doing some of the things they tried to pull on me. If I had tried what some of them did in school, I would be sent down to the principal's office for the wood. My new friend Bob said, "Frank, you have to develop techniques that the students will follow. You have to put the fear of God into them. Do not send anyone down to the office. They don't want to see these kids."

There were probably more than a few times—more than I would like to admit—when I didn't have classroom control. However, I very quickly learned some of the classroom do-nots. For example, I thought it would be nice if the kids had a small Christmas celebration in the shop. After all, what could go wrong? I didn't know this was against school policy. A staff handbook– of the do's and don'ts for the staff – was in process but didn't exist yet.

During that Christmas celebration, one of my students asked me, "Mr. A., can I go out to my car and get something?"

"Sure," I said.

He came back into the shop, slipped on the floor, a six-pack fell out of his coat and broken glass and beer sloshed on the body-shop floor. Yikes—clean it up quick!

Another memorable experience I had was when I planned a field trip to the Cadillac Fleetwood assembly plant in downtown Detroit, Michigan. While we were waiting to board the bus, a strong smell of burning upholstery wafted down from the second floor of the storage area in the shop. I climbed the ladder to find out what was burning, and I saw three seniors smoking marijuana. The look in their eyes said it all.

I said to them, "Wait until we come back, you mother scratchers. You will not graduate!"

Throughout the entire field trip, they were very quiet and didn't say much. I kept thinking, "They were great in class and very talented. How can they be so dumb to do this and embarrass me in front of the class." Everyone wondered what I was going to do. Would I be the guy who would prevent them from graduating? I had their futures in my hands. I thought about it, sent them home after school, and then I had a conference with each of them and their parents on an individual basis. I gave each of them after-school duties in the body shop. They graduated on time, and I learned another technique about classroom management during my first year.

Oh, that first year—what a ride it was for me!

Mr. Bully

Another first-year experience that stays burned in my mind forever was the first time a bully physically challenged me. This classroom bully threatened to beat my ass. I had the usual class clowns and tough guys who wouldn't listen to me or anyone. They were always looking for the easy way out, wanting to show everyone how tough they were.

This punk kid, who was about six foot two and a former football player, had been thrown off the team for insubordination. Now he was in my auto-body program. I would instruct him to do this, and he would do that. It was a game for this big guy, and I wasn't about to play his game.

I counted the days until the first quarter card marking was coming to an end. I knew the grade Mr. Big would be receiving. He had earned the famous three-pronged letter E. My day would finally be here. I'd show this wise guy I wasn't fooling around. I called him to my office to review his grade for the first quarter. I was actually excited and thrilled to inform him he was receiving a failing grade of E. I wished I had a camera with me to snap a photo of the expression on his face. The macho punk came to life as I finally got his attention. This is what was said at the conference:

"Kevin, how do you think you did this card marking?"

He said, "I should be getting a B or a C."

I said, "B or C? Are you serious?" I reviewed his daily grades with him, and reminded him that he could do much better if he applied himself. I further explained to him there was no need to be so disruptive and nonproductive in class, and then said to him that his grade will be an E.

He then said, "I ought to kick your fricking ass."

I said, "You want to do what?"

He said, "You heard me."

I then said to him, "Let's go into the classroom right now."

I began thinking, "I can't let this punk kid think I am afraid of him, because I'm not." I didn't even blink an eye as he spoke to me. There was no way I would change his grade. If I did that, all of the kids who had worked so hard would be very upset, and I would be finished for the next thirty weeks of school. I had to think quickly.

I forgot that I was a schoolteacher and threw the rule book out the window. I kept thinking what my good friend Bob had said to me: "No paddle. Do not send any of your kids to the main office for any reason. If you do this, you will show weakness. You are in control of your own classroom management."

If I were to change his grade to pass him, he would brag to his buddies, and my classroom control would be diminished to a big ZERO. Here I was, twenty-five years old and in excellent physical condition. I said to him, "I will probably get fifteen years in prison for what I am about to do to you. Then I will be forty years old, and I will have to start my life over, but I will not take any bullshit from a punk like you."

He looked at me, and I said, "Let's go, punk." I opened the body-shop door. "I will make an example out of you today. You probably didn't think today would be your last day on earth. I said, "Let's go, punk!" I held the door open for him to walk through. I couldn't tell by the look in his eyes whether he was going to cry from fear or if he was pumped up from adrenaline and ready to rumble. I said once again, "LET'S GO!"

He then said to me, "Can I talk to you for a minute?"

"What do you want?" I said.

"Mr. A, do you think if I worked harder in class and stopped being disruptive, my grade would be higher next marking period?"

I said, "Of course it will. But I want to send a clear message to you. Be careful of the words you choose and how you choose to use them when you are talking to someone. These words can come back in a detrimental way that will have severe consequences. There is always someone bigger and tougher than you are. I was hired fresh out of the real world, and my background is very different from that of your average teacher. I would rather be killed or put in the hospital than back down from a punk kid like you. All I want to do is be a good teacher by helping you grow and succeed after graduation."

I went on to say to Kevin, "I will not be reporting this incident to the main office. Respect is a two-way street. Do I make myself clear? Now get your ass back into that class and get moving."

The C Group

Oh my, my first year of teaching was full of new and exciting experiences. A few days before my new students arrived, a neatly dressed lady walked up to me in my classroom and said, "Are you Mr. Antonucci?"

I said, "Yes."

She went on to say, "I am Mrs. Oglethorpe, your special-needs student advocate. Here are the files for all of your special-needs students." She handed me about thirty-five manila file folders filled with carbon copies identifying in detail the backgrounds of students who had special needs and left. I immediately left my classroom with the folders and walked down to Bob's classroom. (Mrs. Oglethorpe spent a whole five minutes with me that morning, and I didn't see her again until the beginning of the second marking period, the eleventh week of school.)

I asked Bob, "What are these folders used for?"

Bob said, "Those are the profiles of your special-needs students."

I thought, *"Profiles?"* I asked Bob, "Profiles for what?"

Bob said, "Have you opened and read them?"

"No."

"Frankie, read them. It will blow your mind."

I read through them quickly and soon began to have flashbacks to that old familiar C group. My teachers had kept a file on me and knew all along I was in the C group. The reality of the system began to sink in. I'd been part of the broken system. But I was on the other side now, and I was the teacher and about to be teaching to the A, B, and C groups. I didn't want to identify them or place them in special areas or rows as I had been placed in elementary school.

I began to read their profiles and didn't like what I was reading. In the third and fifth grade, one student had difficulties reading. Or in grades one through three, another student had difficulties sounding out vowels and words. I didn't want to stereotype these kids as I had been. So, I created a file for each student with his name on it, inserted those manila profile folders and reviewed them only if there was a reason for me to do so. What a student had done, what his learning level had been in elementary years and early on in middle school, was not really relevant in my shop class's eleventh and twelfth graders. I didn't see any pages with room for maturation, growth, and improvement.

It appeared these folders were used to maintain records for additional federal government funding. If a student couldn't read, do math or write a sentence, how and why was he passed and promoted year after year?

I kept reminding myself these were eleventh- and twelfth-grade students I was teaching, not third- and fourth-graders. How and why did they end up in high school without the necessary skills of reading, writing, and math? I couldn't believe it. I began to realize how I had gotten through school. Keep quiet, lie low, do not cause any trouble and you will receive social promotion. Kids are quick to figure out the system. I was now learning how the system worked.

I had let my childhood friend Vincent down, and I promised God I would never do that again. My classroom demeanor was to treat all of my students at the same level. I was not about to play favorites or demonstrate special treatment because of their previous grade levels. There were a few students who needed to have special accommodations; yet I kept everything on a normal level and didn't single these kids out. I gave those few who needed assistance either tailored lessons or assigned them to work with a partner during the hands-on part of the program.

If my lesson was too difficult for a student, I would go into my office and review his manila file. I could seek out additional help if necessary, and address the issue with Mrs. Oglethorpe, the student, and the parents of the student so we could figure out how to best teach him.

My sole purpose was to teach, mentor, guide, and be a good role model for every student. The reality is that after the graduation parties had ended and the sound of horns blaring from their cars had stopped, my students would be facing the cold, hard world, either enrolling in to a college or pounding the pavement looking for a job and fitting into the working world. I wanted to give them 100 percent – to teach them the work ethic and survival skills they needed to become successful. I would not become a teacher who would socially promote them just because I didn't want to deal with their parents and the main office.

I imagined seeing my former students in the real world, and I didn't ever want hear them to say to me, "Thanks, Mr. A. I didn't learn a thing in your class. Why did you pass me?"

Meetings...Too Late

I was proud and honored that I had been given the opportunity to become a teacher. I believed in the phrase "No Child Left Behind" before it became popular. To me it meant that a teacher should examine a student's potential and tailor the teaching so that the student could learn, rather than give the student a passing grade based on social promotion.

Periodically, I attended scheduled meetings regarding individual special-needs students. These meetings consisted of approximately five or six people. Each of the attendees had his or her own agenda, to rubber-stamp the meeting to cover everyone's asses. I was amazed. Some were genuinely concerned for the students becoming successful, and the rest were clock watchers who wanted to speed the meeting up in order to beat the traffic out of the parking lot. I will always remember those rubber – stampers.

I believed all educators should focus on helping these kids become successful. I knew education was no different than any other business or industry. There were those who did their jobs with the passion of seeing the kids succeed, and those who were there just for the paycheck. Thank God, the majority were there for the kids.

Ronnie

I had one quiet young man in my program who was timid, shy and soft spoken. He was only five foot three and his name was Ronnie. He was smaller than the average seventeen- to eighteen-year-old senior. However, his size didn't keep him from participating in class 100 percent on a regular basis.

Ronnie didn't dress to be cool. He was a well-groomed boy and quietly kept to himself, although I could see he wanted to fit in and be one of the guys. He rarely asked me any questions and always followed my directions to the letter. Once in a while, I would say something funny to him just to see him give me a partial smile, because most of the time the expression on his face was very serious.

I looked through Ron's manila folder and was taken back. His reading was third- or fourth-grade level, and his math and English were not much better. His verbal communication skills were at an all-time low. Here we were: Ronnie was a special-needs student in his senior year of high school, and turning eighteen years old to boot. I said to myself, "He will never survive in the real world." Ronnie was in my first twelfth-grade graduating class. He had been passed through the system as a number, not a person. I couldn't change his previous eleven years of schooling. What was I going to do?

I could pass him and let someone else worry about him, or I could try to retain him for another year of training with me. Retaining him would enable me to build his confidence and teach him basic skills to help him become successful. I began to interact more with Ron and could sense he didn't have much self-confidence. His motor and academic skills were below the fourth or fifth grade. I remembered Vincent, and I kept thinking, "How will this kid make it in the real world?"

My first step was to build Ron's self-confidence, and I thought, "If I can get him to be more verbal and smile, this would be a plus for both of us."

In the beginning, Ron was a bit intimidated and rarely interacted with me. I tried to get him to smile, but this was difficult. Gradually, I gave Ron small tasks that I knew he could accomplish without too much difficulty. I started to see a change in him, and he appeared to be more open with me. Doing auto-body work would be a challenge for him however he had the ability to become an automotive detailer. If he learned to do detailing he'd feel successful and could earn a living. I designed Ron's academic and performance grades around his capabilities. Therefore, he could pass my class because failing him would only keep him in a dark place for the rest of his life. Ronnie needed an overdue boost of self-confidence.

No one enjoys or derives satisfaction from failure. It is our nature to want praise and to be positively reinforced as we continue to grow in life. My students ranged from fifteen to eighteen years of age and I wondered how many had been praised in a positive manner, and how many were not. We may not admit it, but as we reflect on our own experiences, we can see that we all need that proverbial pat on the back.

I set out to build Ron's self-esteem and give him the confidence he was craving but didn't have much more time to do this. Forty weeks of school seems like a long time, but when you are teaching someone life skills, the time moves past in a blur. Ronnie was passing my class based on his skill level, not on his academic performance or maturity level.

Because Ronnie was classified as a special-needs student, meetings were scheduled throughout the school year, both formal and informal. The meetings began with the same old same old. Mrs. Oglethorpe would begin the meeting, sitting straight and professional in her seat. She was always looking good, I must say—not a hair out of place and wearing the latest New York fashions, ready for a magazine cover shoot.

At this meeting, I was wearing my dusty body-shop clothes. I sat next to Ronnie and his mother, waiting patiently for the meeting to begin. I had paper and a pencil in front of me, ready to take copious notes about Ronnie's future.

We sat patiently waiting for Ronnie's sending-school counselor to arrive. He was already ten minutes late. Suddenly the door opened, and in walked a man with a pipe hanging from his mouth. His appearance was a sharp contrast to Mrs. Oglethorpe's. This disheveled guy looked as if he were homeless. He introduced himself to me. As he shook my hand, I could see the yellow nicotine stains on his fingers, and smell the strong aroma of stale pipe smoke. He was an awful sight to see. He called himself a professional? Not too impressive. He began reviewing Ronnie's grades and briefly discussed Ronnie's training after he graduated from high school.

I said, "Graduating from high school?" Prior to this exit meeting, I had conferenced with Ronnie and his mother and made a strong suggestion that he should be retained in high school for one more year. I told them that one extra year would really enhance his confidence and give him a better

156

chance of succeeding. Ronnie and his mother were in agreement. Now, in this meeting, his counselor began reviewing Ronnie's other grades and the grades I had given him based on his capabilities.

"I see, Mr. Antonucci that Ron is doing very well in your program, and he has passed the last three quarters."

I said, "That is correct. However, I am making a strong recommendation to this committee that Ron should be retained to repeat his senior year of high school. He is not ready to graduate this year."

Ron's mother appeared to be overwhelmed with the educational jargon and acronyms and didn't say much on Ron's behalf. The questions were now addressed to me because Ron was in my class for three hours every day.

"Mr. Antonucci, what can you tell us about Ron's performance? How's he doing?"

I said, "Ron has grown immensely, although his skill level remains at the lower end. However, he continues to grow socially, and his communication skills have improved. He is not at the confidence level I would like to see if he has to go to work after he graduates. I recommend that Ron be retained for another full year of high school. I have previously discussed this with Ron and his mother, and they agree this will give Ron a greater opportunity to succeed after he graduates."

The committee began to ask of me, "How can we retain Ron? He has all passing grades in your class."

As I stated earlier, Ron had entered my class with low self-esteem and minimum hands-on skills. If I hadn't made the classroom accommodations for him, Ron would not have passed my class and would continue to feel defeated and might give up on himself. The committee went on to say, "What you say is true. However, there is nothing we can do at this time, and he is scheduled to graduate in June."

I was furious and felt terrible for Ron and his mother. I saw the look of disappointment in their eyes. The committee said, "There is a county program for Ron, and he will be eligible for additional training." However, I knew that the county did not have an automotive program, but Ron might be able to learn how to do basket weaving. Then they looked at their wristwatches and said, "Wow! it's already 1:55 p.m. I have an appointment after school today. Ron, do you have any questions for us?"

Ronnie said, "Uh, uh, no."

"How about you, Mom? Do you have any questions for us?"

The woman hung her head, looked at the table, and shook her head no.

That was a sad day for me, and I felt defeated. I couldn't help Ron because I had given him passing grades in the hopes of building up his self-confidence. What a slap in my face.

After Ronnie graduated that year, I never saw him again. The end of my first year of teaching was truly a learning experience for me. As we often say to ourselves, "We learn from our mistakes." How true this is.

Summertime at the Lincoln Dealer

During my first year of teaching, Chris and I went through many challenges and changes in our lives: the closing of National Body Repair, bankruptcy, and a new job. There were many financial challenges too. Although I was now receiving a steady income, I had bills, and more bills more than I cared to admit to. Bankruptcy does not discharge monies that are owed to the state and federal governments, and I still had my attorney's fees. Throughout the unthinkable process, I was able to keep our home.

However, I faced new challenges. My new job required me to enroll in a college to begin work on my bachelor's degree. There was no way I was going to ask my father-in-law for financial tuition assistance. I had assured him I would pay him back the $10,000 he had loaned me four and a half years earlier. He never pressured me or discussed the money with me; he knew I would pay him back one day.

I never got over the feeling of guilt, and I lost my self-confidence that I'd be a good businessman. I was so embarrassed I rarely went out, in fear that someone would point a finger at me and say, "Look! There's Frank Antonucci! He went bankrupt and shafted a lot of people. He used to own National Body Repair!"

I was angry at myself that I hadn't taken the advice of all of the experienced people who had tried to help me. I was ashamed because I couldn't save the business. One day, I ran into my old landlord, Pete, who had tried over and over to give me some business tips, and I just didn't get it.

He said, "Hey, Frank. How are you doing?"

Sheepishly I said, "OK, Pete."

"What's wrong?"

"I feel horrible I didn't listen to you or anyone else, and I feel horrible for filing bankruptcy on everyone, especially those who trusted me."

Pete said, "You are only twenty-five years old and still wet behind the ears. You need to get over it. You need to

159

think about your family, not what people will be saying about you. You did what you had to do, and you have to look ahead for brighter days. Frank, look ahead."

"Thanks, Pete. I will finally take your advice" I meant it! I started moving forward and stopped feeling sorry for myself.

My last day of school was June 18, 1976, and I felt, as Alice Cooper once sang, "School is out for summer." Teachers had the option of getting paid only through the school year or through the summer break. I chose to be paid through only the school year. By doing this, my net monthly pay increased, but I wouldn't receive a paycheck during the summer break, and still needed to provide an income for our family to live on. Money was tight; however, we made it through our first summer break. I spent many long hours working in a body shop. I was also offered a painter's position at a Lincoln dealership in Detroit and I gladly accepted it. I was paid on commission and received 50 percent of the labor. The more cars I painted, the more money I made. It was unbelievable! This was a high-volume dealer, and there were plenty of cars to be painted. I loved painting, and I loved the paychecks too. I worked for approximately seven hard and long weeks. I earned enough money that summer to support us and to dig myself out of some of my debt, so the family could take a trip to California. We had a great time. I began to climb the mountain and had hope once again.

September and Labor Day were quickly approaching, and I needed to get ready to return to my teaching position. I couldn't wait to begin my second year and see my students who were returning for Auto-Body Shop II. I'd also meet the new students who were beginning Auto-Body Shop I.

Teaching, Year Two

I believed that when teaching and preparing students for the real world, an instructor should understand the current industry standards and trends. Some teachers reused the same old material. The students would figure that out, and tell other students and friends, "Take this class. That teacher teaches the same material that my older brother had four years ago, and he gave me his notes. You can borrow them from me."

I never wanted to teach my classes that way. I wanted new and exciting lessons each year to stimulate enthusiasm and create excitement in my classroom. The core of the program remained the same, but the classroom projects continued to pose challenges for everyone, including me.

My second year of teaching would be more of a challenge for me. I had three major commitments I needed to be mindful of: first was to my own family, the second was to work on my bachelor's degree, and the third was to maintain the best learning environment for my students to meet their needs.

Our grading system was designed for student success, not failure. I had different types of students in my class, both high-academic-level students as well as low-academic students. Some were the kind who could read and understand the textbook from cover to cover but couldn't perform the tasks to pass the hands-on portion of the program. Others had difficulties in academics but could pass the hands-on portion with flying colors. There were also students who had given up on themselves and had passed into the eleventh grade through the social-promotion process.

I used this method and technique to teach a typical hands-on lesson to my class: I began by saying in a loud, clear voice with a smile on my face, "Good morning, class. How's everyone doing today? Are you ready to learn today? Good! Let's get going." I wanted a relaxed and structured classroom environment that was conducive for all learners. Next, I took the daily attendance and held the students accountable for either being tardy or absent on the previous day. Then, we would discuss the previous lessons in a broad matter. A quick review helped me to jump-start the program in a positive way. I strived for open communication; it was a great tool to build trust between my students and myself. I would ask questions to keep them thinking and prepared to learn the daily lesson.

I'd announce a lesson and ask them to pay attention and stay awake. "Today, I will show you how to use a pick hammer and remove a small dent. Bring your stools over to the demo area and get your notebooks and pencils. I want you to write down the key highlights, since you will be seeing this on your next test." I'd visually show them as I explained and demonstrated the proper use of the most commonly used hammer in the body-shop business: the pick hammer.

I used words that the class could easily understand about the uniqueness and design of this hammer. "The flat end of this hammer is used to straighten and restore the flat surfaces of the damaged body panel. On the opposite end, you will see a sharp pointed tip. This is used to remove the low areas caused by the impact. I notice that some of you are not writing down the key parts of my demonstration. Is there a reason why? I want to remind all of you that you will see these key words on a test in the near future. I will permit you to use the notes from your notebooks during the test. Therefore I strongly suggest that you write something down for future references. AM I MAKING MYSELF CLEAR TO EVERYONE?" I'd finish in a loud voice.

I weighed the hands-on part of a test more heavily than the written portion because the actual body work involved hands-on skills this was far more than important than the written portion. However, I had to hold them accountable for both. Prior to a test, I would quickly review the hands-on demo and the key terms.

My students were given four to five weeks to prepare for the hands-on test during the regular class period. As they practiced the lesson, I walked about the classroom, going from student to student to be sure everyone was on task. For example, to complete one task during a test, the students had to perform the five steps of auto-body work that I'd taught during the first card marking period. They could either do a step or not know how to do it and so, would either pass or fail each step; no maybes.

I did take into consideration each student on an individual basis. If the student had coordination issues, I made accommodations so that he could pass. I'd evaluate him on the process and procedures, but not necessarily hold him accountable for accuracy.

I remember my own ninth-grade machine-shop class. One of our class requirements was to sharpen a one-eighth drill bit. I tried over and over to get it right for a passing grade. Each time I would sharpen it, I would bring it up to my teacher for a grade, and he'd say, "Not good enough. Do it again."

"Will you show me one more time?" I asked.

"Not now. I want to finish the sports section." He was reading the *Detroit Free Press* at his desk.

I asked one of my buddies, "Did you turn in your drill bit for a grade?"

"Yes," he said.

"What grade did you get?" I asked.

He said, "I got an A."

"Will you sharpen mine?"

He agreed. He sharpened my drill bit, and I turned it in and got an A too. My teacher never knew that I didn't sharpen my own drill bit. I finally learned how to sharpen a drill bit when I was about twenty-two years old.

That is why I developed my hands-on testing method. I never wanted any of my students to slip through my class and not learn a thing from me. Every now and then, I had a complaint or two, saying I was too tough a teacher and too rigid, and the hands-on testing was unfair. I just took it on the chin and kept doing the hands-on testing method throughout my teaching career. It was effective and accurate too.

I had learned an important lesson: teachers have to be held accountable for the subject they are teaching, the student has to be held accountable for the learning, and the parents need to support the teacher and their children too.

The lesson I learned from Ronnie will forever be burned into my mind. Many of my students were accustomed to being passed and not being held to a higher standard. If a student received a passing grade, we would never hear from the parents, and the students would not complain. They would be satisfied with passing and unconcerned about what they learned.

That's fine for some but not acceptable for those teachers, like me, who really wanted to make a difference with their students. I never want to run into a former student and have him say to me, "I didn't learn anything in your class, and you passed me just to move me through the system." We wanted every one of our students to succeed. I wanted Ronnie to spend another year learning so he could be successful, and I failed at doing so. Never again. So I took a look at our grading process.

Students Manipulating the System

Each letter grade has assigned a number of points attached to it, beginning with an A+ that is worth thirteen points. The letter grade A worth twelve, and so on down the line until you got to E, which was worth zero.

Final grades were calculated thus: First quarter equaled 20 percent. Second quarter equaled 20 percent. Midterm exam was 10 percent. Third quarter was 20 percent. Fourth quarter was 20 percent, and the final exam was 10 percent.

However, the students discovered a major loophole in the calculations. I will describe how clever students can be. They had the system figured out before we did. They were creative and knew the system inside and out.

This is a typical example of the methods these students used to manipulate the grading system. All seems to be going well, and I say to myself, "I am blessed to have a great group of students." There's one student especially, who appears friendly, task orientated, punctual, and interested in the program. I believe I have a student here to learn and become successful.

This student appears to be working at his potential and is following the classroom criteria. He is an excellent student to have in class. On his first card marking this student received an A that is worth twelve points.

At the beginning of the second card- marking period, the same student begins to act out, have behavioral issues, slacks off in his performance, and begins to fall short of the classroom expectations. Therefore on his second card marking period he receives a C+ (six points). He is now ready to take his mid-term exam and he receives a C- (four-points).

After the midterm exams have been taken we begin the third card marking period. This same student begins to become a discipline problem and will not follow the classroom policies, disrupts others and causes trouble – resulting in many phone calls to his parents and numerous trips to the Principal's office. I warn this student he will not pass my class if he continues to be disruptive and not follow the classroom rules.

I began to reason with him with hopes of turning him around. Therefore on his third card marking period grade I gave a D- (one-point). I am not sure the student can continue to be in class.

We are now in the fourth card marking period and the student has run out of opportunities to pass and receives an E (zero-points) and still doesn't care about passing. The student says to me, "You can't fail me, and there is nothing you're going to do to me. You can't withhold my credits."

This hit me like a ton of bricks. The student was correct. I couldn't do a thing about it and he will receive his three credits and I would be on the losing end of this year-long battle. The student was well aware of the system and there is no way he can lose his credits or fail my class now, so he doesn't have to try. He gets a D- (one point) for the third card marking, and a D- (one-point) on his final exam. Averaging the student's accumulative points using the thirteen point scale the student's final grade for the entire year was a soft D, and he passed the class.

I realized I had given up the farm in the first card marking. Once I'd given the student an A on the first report card I would be at a disadvantage for the rest of the school year, and he would pass the class no matter what he did the rest of the year (almost). I didn't have a trump card. This final outcome was an example of how the students were in control, not the teacher. It was also a mockery of the system, and I wouldn't have tolerated it—if I had figured it out before the students did.

In Ron's case during my first year, I couldn't retain him because the system said his grades were passing, but for different circumstances. I said it, and I will say it again: my first year was a learning year, and some of those kids ate me up and spit me out. I knew it and couldn't do anything about it. My hands were tied. Well, fool me once, but not twice. My classroom management and my grading system would become bulletproof in my second year of teaching. It was my time to take control of the classroom.

Second Year Meet and Greet

On the first day of the new school year, I welcomed my returning second-year students and my new first-year students into the classroom. We talked about our summer vacation experiences, which was a good way to help them ease back into school mode. At the end of that class period, I said to my students, "Tomorrow, I will give you a handout about what we will be doing this year, and my classroom guidelines."

My friend Bob and I wanted to be in a win-win situation with our students, so we had developed a new classroom grading scale for a number of reasons, the most important were classroom management and a structured learning environment. Our new scale changed the old thirteen point grading system into a new five-hundred point grading scale.

The Five-Hundred-Point Scale

The new grading system started on the second day of the new school year. I explained our new five-hundred point grading system that reversed the former process. All students would receive five hundred points (which equaled an A). My hands-on test equaled fifty percent of their grade, taking notes in their notebooks equaled twenty-five percent and written tests equaled twenty-five percent. I gave examples of how this new system will work and answered their questions.[14]

---

[14] I knew a major change like this needed to start at the beginning of the school year because otherwise, I'd have endless conferences with the parents and school principal about why I changed things around.

Students couldn't earn any points, but they could lose them. I put the reasons they could lose points in my class syllabus. I asked them to take the syllabus home, read it, review it with their parents, and then have their parents sign a section that the students would return to me.

To keep their points (and not lose them), they would have to do things like be in class every day and be on time and maintain a positive attitude. I asked them, "If you're not here how can you learn?" At the end of each card marking period' I met with each student individually to discuss their scores, strong points and where they needed to improve. This kept our communication channels open.

I explained how my new grading system worked. Every student who was enrolled in my program started with an A. When I made this announcement, I heard my students talking among themselves, saying, "Is he trying to fool us? Is he kidding around?"

I said, "No, this is for real, and I am not kidding around." I explained it.

"The objective is for you to keep the five hundred points that you currently have. To keep them and receive an A on your report card, you must follow the classroom rules as written on your handout. You are now in the eleventh and twelfth grades and it's time you are held accountable for what you do or don't do. You are in charge of your own destiny."

I next read aloud each and every classroom rule as written, one at a time, with clear examples. The students asked about how they'd lose points so I told them. "Being tardy to class would be minus ten points for every minute late. Not staying on task would lose a student twenty-five points. Talking or sleeping during my hands-on demonstrations was minus twenty-five points" . . . I felt this technique would be an excellent method for me to maintain classroom control and grade each student fairly.

Whenever students lost points, I would remind them and give them a warning. I marked those deductions in my grade book in pencil – which I might erase later.

At first, everyone kept their A's. By the beginning of the third week of school, the honeymoon period ended, and some students acted out to test my system. I took those students who lost points into my office, explained to them why they had lost points and reminded them to get it together fast. Most understood I was serious about this and improved, but there were a few who still wanted to test my point system and refused to comply with the classroom rules in my handout. They would find out! We all learn from our mistakes—some faster than others.

C.P.C. Auto Body class of 1983

I wanted my classroom to be fun, meaningful and most of all, orderly to allow all my students to learn. I didn't want to repeat my first year of teaching and have the students in

170

control and my hands tied because of ineffective classroom strategies. I reminded myself, "I am in control, and I will have control." I realized my students would make mistakes, and most would learn from the first and maybe second warning that they were in danger of losing points, and that the consequences would be a lower grade for the first quarter.

As we moved into the seventh and eighth weeks of school, I began to prepare them for their hands-on test. They would be tested on the five important steps taught earlier in the marking period. Throughout the marking period, the students were given classroom time to practice every important step. I walked about the classroom and individually helped every student to develop a technique and method of his own. The five steps were either right or wrong. There were no maybes. The students who thought they could beat me and my system were surprised. The rules of the game had now changed. There were no more fun and games in my classroom. It was time to get down to business, and I had the classroom-control ball in my court.

I was brutal in the first card-marking period. Out of seventy-two students, the grades were as follows: no A's, no B's, ten C's, twenty-five D's, and thirty-seven E's. This was a shake-up for everyone – students, parents, the main office and the special-education department.

Before the report-card grades were recorded and sent to the counselor to be processed, I reviewed every student's grade with him on a one-to-one basis. I reminded all the students what they needed to do to bring their grades up and pass my class. Most agreed, and some reminded me of the extra credit they had completed in the hopes of raising their grade. I listened and asked them for a commitment to the program. I said, "If I raise your grade, where is your commitment?" I did this to give them a sense of being responsible for their own individual actions. They promised me they would work hard, and not disappoint me and their classmates by demonstrating a positive attitude in becoming a team player.

My main goal was to prepare them for the real outside world of work. In the second card-marking period, the students' attitudes began to improve, and I saw them growing from boys into young men. As I watched them mature, I was proud to be their teacher.

The new five-hundred-point scale was effective and working in my classroom. I began to see the students performing like well-oiled machines. I had created a structured learning environment, and an excellent classroom management system was in place. As I approached the end of my second year of teaching, I had a feeling of accomplishment that I hadn't had at the end of my first year. Everyone passed, and the students knew their boundaries. I was deeply committed to my students and never wanted to repeat the experience I'd had with Ronnie during my first year.

Developing a Connection

I didn't want to become complacent and get stuck in a routine or a rut delivering the same old material year after year. So, during our summer breaks, I continued to work in the collision industry, learning current methods and techniques. At the beginning of each school year, I welcomed the students back, and I told them what I'd learned during my summer hands-on jobs.

Connecting with the students was always critical. I continuously searched for automotive projects of interest for the students to work on. Student buy-in was necessary to develop a sense of pride and ownership. Sometimes as I introduced a new lesson, the students asked "Why do we need to know this stuff? Who needs this junk?" I told them, "You need to learn it and here is why . . ."

My lessons had two parts. First, I would teach the students the reason why, and second, I would show them how to do it. Hands-on training teaches the students the how's and why's by seeing the lesson performed along with a clear explanation of its purpose. I saw the expressions on their faces change as if I were a magician doing a magic show. All eyes focused on me. I demonstrated how to repair a damaged fender as I continued to show that the concepts they may have learned in geometry and physics classes could be applied to designing and working on the automobiles.

Many of my students learned best by watching what I did, then doing what I'd had shown them by using their hands to do the same things. I soon discovered my students learned best by watching what I did, then learning to use their hands to do the same things. It was amazing to see the students discover they had problem-solving skills and didn't know it. I saw them develop pride and confidence as they worked. It was truly a blessing to watch this. I kept reminding them I was proud that they had become mature and confident in themselves, and I also reminded them that in the real world, no one will babysit or spoon-feed them along the way.

A Typical Day in the Classroom

Hands-On Learning Styles

As I became more experienced in the classroom, I began to learn more about the many different methods that enabled me to become an effective teacher. Some people learn best by listening, some by watching, and others by doing. (These are called "learning styles[15].") Many teachers themselves learned best by listening and then doing what they have been taught. However, if a kid is a hands-on learner, like I was, he or she learns best by doing. When I taught, I demonstrated a procedure as my students watched, then had them use their hands to do what I'd shown them. Showing and telling them was not enough. They needed to *do* the lesson to really

---

[15] The seven learning styles are *Visual* (spatial):You prefer using pictures, images, and spatial understanding; *Aural* (auditory-musical): You prefer using sound and music; *Verbal* (linguistic): You prefer using words, both in speech and writing; *Physical* (kinesthetic): You prefer using your body, hands and sense of touch; *Logical* (mathematical): You prefer using logic, reasoning and systems; *Social* (interpersonal): You prefer to learn in groups or with other people; and *Solitary* (intrapersonal): You prefer to work alone and use self-study.

understand it. After all, auto body work is definitely a hands-on job that people *do*.

Here are some examples of the learning (and doing) styles. How many of us have made a purchase only to discover the item needed to be assembled? We hope we can do it correctly. We all have different ways of going about this process.

Let's take a look at a person we'll call Larry. Larry is a college-educated engineer and a problem-solver. He has purchased a new gas barbeque grill. He opens the box and carefully removes and organizes the parts. He begins to read the instructions step by step, and suddenly realizes there is an extra part. He is unable to locate where it goes. After a few calls to the manufacturer, the issue isn't being resolved. Larry then decides to complete the assembly, only to discover the manufacturer made the error upon packaging the item. He may be thinking, "Never again will I purchase an item from them that will require assembly." He is able to complete the assembly, and cook his burgers.

Some people identify with Larry?

A second person is Tony, who is a hands-on guy. Tony and his wife purchase a new lawnmower. On the cover of the box is a big color picture of the mower, with the instructions clearly written and a notice saying "Assembly required." Tony arrives at home, tears the box open, and sorts the parts on a table. Tony is an outstanding mechanic but barely made it through high school. He takes pride in his work and is excellent with his hands-on skills. He is nearly finished with the assembly when he finds a mysterious part. He cannot figure out where or how it attaches to the mower. Tony uses the picture and directions on the box to finish the assembling.

Tony uses his mechanical knowledge and experience, and refers to the picture and instructions when necessary.

Can you identify with Tony?

Larry and Tony approach tasks differently, but both get them done. A good teacher will identify each student's learning style to connect with that student. In a class of seventy students, all might have similar ways of learning, but have different personalities.

It is imperative that teachers connect with their students, be role models and be honest, fair, and have reasonable expectations. Good teachers laugh, listen, and, most of all, admit to their students when they are wrong. Educators sometimes forget students can see right through them. Kids know when adults are not being honest or up-front with them. I realize that every teacher cannot develop a personal relationship with every student, but can be understanding and listen to each of their needs and not play favorites.

Identifying students' different learning styles is essential for teachers to reach their students. All of us remember the best (or worst) teachers we had.

As a teacher, I continually stressed the importance of academics: reading, writing and arithmetic. These are essential tools for making it in the real world. I also taught them the importance of getting along with others in the work place.

My program was an elective and was taught at a satellite building within the school district. The students chose to take it. I often told my students that being an excellent auto-body person isn't enough, but having a great attitude and being respectful to others are necessary too."

They Will Never Forget

Autorama

I always looked for automotive projects that my students (fifteen-to-eighteen-year-olds) had a passion for: cool cars like Corvettes, Mustangs, GTOs, 'Cudas, motorcycles. Those vehicles got them involved. I also wanted to promote my students, let the world see how great these kids were. In most schools, only athletes or high academic achievers are recognized. Hands-on students are often overlooked. I thought, "This is not the way it should be." Our culture needs people who can repair automobiles, furnaces, and do plumbing. We need people who can build and make things. I began to explore avenues to promote my students.

When I had entered my 1964 Ford in the Detroit Autorama, it gave me a whole different perspective on life. It was a real boost to my self-confidence. I wanted my students to experience the same success and learn the true meaning of teamwork. I explained what the Autorama was, and shared my personal experience. I brought pictures of my 1964 Ford and passed them around the classroom. I asked my class if they would want to do a project like this.

I needed one hundred percent commitment from my students. I went into to detail and explained the multipurpose for doing this project. Number one was to improve their hands-on skills and number two was to reinforce their self-worth to become productive, desirable employees. I wanted these kids to be recognized and be successful. This wasn't for me, it was for them. I was excited to see the enthusiasm within the classroom. Many of them had never entered into any kind of competition. Excitement was in the air.

I assigned specific tasks for every student in the class. I explained how we would be counting on each one of them to follow very specific directions. "If we want to win a trophy with our entry, we must be united and apply ourselves 100 percent," I said.

I wanted to use each student's strengths in the best possible way. The class began to explode into enthusiasm. They had something to look forward to—building our first Detroit Autorama winner.

I carefully placed the students into groups and assigned each group to work on specific components of the car. I made sure every student worked on tasks that he was best at. This gave them a feeling of confidence and pride, and was a great morale builder. I explained to them that their teamwork was like being in the NBA All-Star game or the Super Bowl.

Some did bodywork, some painted. Some did preparation work and detail, others built the display or filled out the necessary paper work. Each person was important; the project depended on everyone. "All hands on deck!" I'd say if one group failed to follow through.

I also reminded them of the importance of maintaining their attendance and grades. I almost didn't graduate because my focus was on building my first show car and I didn't want this show car preventing them from graduating. It was time to put the team into action to build their first Detroit Autorama winner.

We worked out a timeline, and were all aware the car had to be finished and in pristine condition. We had approximately ten school weeks to build it and I was confident we'd meet our December 20 deadline. Could we pull this thing off? All we had to do now was find the project car. And we did.

Our entry was a 1966 Corvette Coupe 327 V-8 four-speed, and we'd make it bad to the bone. I was in my second year of teaching and about to take a group of young men on the journey of their lives—being part of a national custom-car event. This would be the first time the public would see what they had learned in my class, and this would give them an opportunity to be a part of a winning team without the use of sporting equipment.

As the completion date grew near, the community came alive: parents, staff members, school board, and so on. The local newspaper featured us on the second front page, and that was a real boost for the students. All eyes were on them and the program. I told the kids that if we won, it would be because of all of them working as a team. Quietly, I know that if we lost, people might say that I was nuts for trying to pull this off. Some people would never let me forget it.

The kids and I put in many after-school hours as the Corvette neared completion. The camaraderie among the students was unbelievably strong. At times, it was hard to believe they were kids; they looked and acted more like a group of grown men. I was so proud of the way they each worked.

The big weekend came. Our Corvette entry had to be taken down to Cobo Hall on the Wednesday before the show. I procured a transporter to bring our car down right after New Year's Day in January 1977. The weather was typical Michigan winter: snow and salt on the roads. We did not want to take the chance of getting our pristine entry dirty.

The students' faces and the faces of the other participants shone with pride as we uncovered our 1966 Corvette entry. It was euphoric and I had tears in my eyes. The students moved the Corvette to our assigned area and began to set up our display. I heard them make decisions about where the signs would be placed. It was great watching them take charge and be responsible.

The show began on a Friday and ended on Sunday— three days in all. I didn't attend the show that weekend. My part had been getting them there. Their part was to enjoy and have fun. Before trophies were awarded on Sunday at 6:00 p.m., I arrived. As I walked up to the car, I saw the kids with their parents, girlfriends, and spectators explaining what part they had worked on and how much fun they had had doing it.

The announcement came: "All show-car participants report with their show card to the main ballroom for the awards ceremony." As the students and I proceeded to the ballroom, tension and anticipation were in the air. We sat patiently and quietly as the awards were announced. The Corvette had been entered in two categories: High School Class and Mild Conservative Sports Class. As the master of ceremonies announced that the second-place winner in the Mild Conservative Sports was our Career Preparation Center, I heard a loud roar from my students. My eyes began to tear up again. The students went up to the podium and accepted the trophy on behalf of their school and their classmates.

Our first Detroit Autorama Entry 1966 Corvette

*Proud monuments class of 1977, winning our First Detroit
Autorama.*

We continued to sit patiently, wondering who would
receive the High School Class awards. The announcement
came: the first-place award was going to *our* Career
Preparation Center for the students' outstanding 1966
Corvette!

The roof came off the place. There was so much
cheering for and recognition of our group of students who
had never before been involved in any type of competition. I
was so proud and humbled to be their teacher!

The Program Keeps Going

During my twenty-four years of teaching this outstanding program, I had students who were male and female, academic achievers and nonacademic achievers, in special education and regular education. In that time, my students won over thirty first-place trophies and built numerous show and muscle cars. 1977 was a good year for two reasons. It was our first year of winning Autorama, and Christine gave birth to our third child. We were blessed with a boy who we named Nicholas Joseph Antonucci.

The feeling of pride and confidence began to appear to a group of students that many had written off as unable to make it in the real world. These were the kids who didn't fit the mold of what society expected them to be.

Team work and Hands-On learning

In 1984, our program was featured in *Corvette News*, a national magazine. There were also numerous newspaper articles about us as I continued to promote these kids through various media, including radio and television. I saw my vision for them become a reality. After my students graduated and went into the real world, I reminded them to come back and share their experiences with me and the new students. I was excited to hear their stories as they began to experience real-life situations in the workplace. Some went on to college, and many were hired in the field of auto-body repair. I loved when they knocked on my classroom door. I was always happy and surprised when they returned and shared their stories.

I remember one young man who came back and said to me, "Mr. A., I didn't want to disappoint you, but I didn't go into the auto-body field. I am driving a garbage truck."

I said to him, "Do you like it?"

"Yes."

"Are you paying your bills?"

"Yes."

"Great! I am proud of you. You are not a disappointment to me. You are working and making a living. Not everyone is cut out to be in the auto-body business."

These kids became adults with a purpose in life, and soon they became spouses and then became parents. Isn't the life cycle great? I felt such personal gratification every time alumni returned and shared their stories with me. Throughout my years, I have seen my vision for these kids become a reality, and I was proud that everyone knew how well Mr. A's kids had done.

Thank you, class.

Growing with my Class

1976-1980

As I understood the many needs of my students, I also continued to work toward my teaching certification. I faced many challenges. I was twenty-seven years old, supporting a wife and three children, paying college tuition and still recovering from my bankruptcy on one salary. My wife, Christine, was very supportive, and we both knew I had to receive my teaching certificate to secure my job so I couldn't spend a lot of time with her or the children.

My workday was 7:00 a.m. to 5:00 p.m. Monday through Friday. My program quickly became very popular, and the word was out. "Take Mr. A's class. He's tough, but you will learn a lot and have fun."

My enrollment grew, and soon an extra session was added to my schedule. This allowed me to work an extended day with an additional class period, very similar to overtime. My salary increased, making me one of the highest-paid teachers in the district and eventually the highest-paid teacher in the state of Michigan.

Three nights a week, at the end of my scheduled workday, I was off to college. As I said earlier, I began teaching with eighteen credit hours toward nothing from the community college, and I needed to earn the proper teaching credentials to maintain my status with the State of Michigan.

A few of our First place Detroit Autorama trophies

My close friend Bob was a great mentor to me, and Chris gave me the confidence I needed to succeed. Remember, schoolwork wasn't my strong point. In the fall of 1976, I enrolled in classes at Macomb County Community College (MCCC). I was sitting in the classroom once again, but this time I wasn't there to play games and be a goofball. The students who were in the classes seemed like kids fresh out of high school—because they were. I attended class prepared. I didn't miss class, and made sure I was always prompt. Seemed strange that I was a teacher going to college to become a teacher.

I still didn't like the idea of being away from my family so much. However, I did what I had to do. The days flew into the nights, and my weekends were filled with homework. I've heard time and time again that nothing comes easy, and that is correct. I wonder who said that.

"Nothing in the world is worth having or worth doing unless it means effort, pain, difficulty... I have never in my life envied a human being who led an easy life. I have envied a great many people who led difficult lives and led them well." — Theodore Roosevelt

At this time we lived in Capac, Michigan, and this was my daily schedule:

- I Leave Capac at 5:30 a.m.
- Drive forty-five miles to CPC.
- Work 7:00 a.m. to 5:00 p.m.
- Drive to MCCC.
- Begin class at 6:00 p.m.
- Drive back to Capac at 11:00 p.m.

In 1977, I transferred to Sienna Heights College in Adrian because the community college could not provide me with the teaching credentials required by the State of Michigan. Me, attending a major university? My friend, Bob, and I drove to Adrian, Michigan, to meet the head of the department of educational instruction. Her name was Sister Eileen Rice. When I met her, I immediately felt relaxed and confident. Sister Eileen made accommodations for me so I could take some classes at other closer colleges also to earn my Bachelors of Science degree in secondary education.

During my summers, on Mondays, Wednesdays, and Fridays, I drove 125 miles to Adrian, and that meant leaving Capac at 6:00 a.m. and returning home at 11:00 p.m. Those were very long days, but worth the effort.

In May of 1980 I finally graduated from Sienna Heights College and received my full teaching certification. My GPA was 3.75; which is considered an 'A' grade. Remember, I was the C student? I continued to prove to myself and everyone else I am no longer a "C" student. In the spring of 1985 I

186

graduated from Michigan State University with a Master's Degree in Secondary Education.

Over the next few years, I continued to revise and improve my quality of teaching. I was never satisfied being a teacher who would become complacent. I remember saying to my students: "I don't want you coming back to visit me and find that I'm teaching this class the same way as when you were a student." I never wanted to get stuck in a pattern of mediocrity.

Every summer I worked in various body shops. I enjoyed this immensely for two excellent reasons. The first was obvious—additional funds for my family. The second was being able to provide my students with updated information and current repair methods. I kept reminding myself, "Do not fall into a rut by teaching the same old, same old." I thank God I was able to do this and still have quality time for my family.

Capac is a small town with a big heart, and it was a great community for our family. The home we purchased there was four thousand square feet and sat on twelve rolling acres. It was an excellent area for a…what else? A body shop!

After we moved and settled in, Chris and I discussed the possibility of building a body-shop for me to work in. We picked out a place to build it, and I had my very own paid-for shop. It was so surreal to me. I remembered the mistakes I had made with National Body Repair, and I didn't want to repeat history. Failure still haunted me, and I wanted to prove to myself I could be successful with this new beginning. This shop was thirty feet by thirty-five feet—big enough to work on three cars at a time.

My friends said to me, "Who will drive fifty miles out to the middle of nowhere to bring a car out here for you to work on?" I ignored them and proceeded with my plan. I got so busy that I actually needed to hire some helpers, so I thought, why not give the students an opportunity to work with me outside of a school setting? And this was the beginning of Mr. A.'s Specialty Shop.

I interviewed and hired those who were willing and able to drive fifty miles each way daily. I paid them by the hour and compensated them for their gas. They enjoyed this as much as I did. They worked in the summer before beginning their senior year of school. I didn't hire them after they graduated because they were capable of earning much more than I could pay them for a forty hour work week along with benefits.

As the summers came to an end, my beautiful wife would say to me, "summer is almost over." That meant we took our family vacations. When we got back, I'd be a little depressed about returning to school. However, as soon as I saw my returning students arrive and as I met the new group, I forgot what I was depressed about. I taught three sessions of students, juniors and seniors, one in the morning, one in the afternoon, and one in the late afternoon.

Auto-body was an elective program taught in a facility formally known as a vocational center; today it is called a career and technical education center. Students in my class had to be enrolled in a comprehensive high school where the academic classes were taught. That school was called a sending high school. Although I strongly believed in my program, I also believed in and supported academic education.

I reminded students of this on a regular basis: "You will not get far in life without a high-school diploma." I encouraged them to do their best at all times and never give up on themselves. I also reminded them of the struggles I had gone through and made sure they knew that nothing would be handed to them.

I told my classes that during the summers, I worked to learn new techniques and methods. I focused on my experiences with my returning seniors who were in their second year of the program. As for the new juniors, I gave them the program in a nutshell. I explained to them that I was there for them and I was the real deal.

They always tested me to see what they could get away with, but after they received their first report card, I made believers out of them, because 80 percent received a grade of D or E.

I'd ask this question: "How many of you had a class and passed it with an A or a B?" A number of hands were raised. "How many of you who received that grade didn't learn anything?" Surprisingly, a number of hands went up again. Then I said, "It would be easier for me to give you an A or B. No one would ever question me about what I was teaching— not even your parents. But here in my class you students, you will work hard for your grades, because in the working world, you will need to work hard for a salary. I want you all to become success stories."

They often called me their drill sergeant. I wanted nothing but the best for my students, and after all, I had made it—they could too. I wanted them to set goals. I often said, "If we reach for the moon and come up with the stars, we are doing great. We should never be satisfied with doing less than what we are capable of doing. Rise above the rest, and show everyone that you can do it—and do it very well!"

I continued to infuse the importance of setting realistic goals in my daily lessons, being positive, and developing a great reputation in the real world. One way to build their reputations was to promote my students and our program with our show car for the Detroit Autorama. I was always excited as I searched for our next cool car to enter into competition. I would discuss my finds with the class to get their feedback and their ideas. "How about a 1967 Pontiac GTO? Or a 1969 Plymouth Roadrunner? Four-wheel drive monster pickup truck?"

Doing this gave my students ownership and stimulated enthusiasm, to have their voices heard. They became stakeholders in the process when I was candid with them and included them in the decision-making process every step of the way. This gave them a purpose to attend my class along with their sending school. They knew if they did not attend their classes at their home school, we would be shorthanded when it came to completing our show car.

I wanted to instill commitment in them. It worked year after year and trophy after trophy. I had fun helping them find themselves. Great times and great memories were made year after year. Oh, how I loved those kids.

My Life Changed Forever

October 8, 1998

Have you ever thought you were indestructible? I believed I was immune and unstoppable, that nothing would bring me down. I was a bad-to-the-bone tough guy, or so I thought. I'd bring cars back from Las Vegas and buy and sell them. These were cool cars that hadn't been all rusted out, and I began flipping them. In the summer of 1998, I brought back a creampuff rust free 1984 Chevrolet El Camino, and the students loved it.

"Wow, Mr. A. No rust!"

It was the beginning of the fifth week of school in early October. The sun was shining, and the smell of fall was in the air. I heard the band practice across the street for the Friday-night football game. It was 4:30 p.m., and I said to my class, as I did every day, "OK, it's cleanup time. Start putting your fenders and tools away. Let's go. Get moving." Cleanup time was done at the end of each session to prepare the space for the next class. The students all had specific duties and responsibilities at the end of each class period: sweeping, emptying the trash, and organizing the car parts.

We finished, said our good-byes, and I reminded them to drive safely. Then I told them I would see them tomorrow. I reflected on my day with my students and I hoped my wife was making my favorite meal—spaghetti. I got into my cool El Camino, buckled up, turned on the tunes, and began to leave the school parking lot. I turned onto Fifteen Mile Road, the same route I drove every day. I stopped at the traffic light on Fifteen and Dodge Park and turned right, heading north toward Romeo. I continued to review the events of the day with my class and the lessons for the next day's class period.

I came up to the red light at Sixteen Mile Road and Dodge Park, waiting to proceed. Before I got to the traffic light at Dodge Park and Plumbrook, I saw that cars were stopped. Suddenly, I heard a screeching of tires behind me and I looked in my left rearview mirror to see what was going on. The car behind me slammed into the back of my El

Camino pickup. My head went through the back window and ricocheted off the steering wheel. I passed out for a moment. When I came to, a witness came up to me and asked, "Are you OK? Your head went through the window just like one of those crash test dummies."

I picked up my cell phone to call my wife and couldn't remember our phone number. However, I remembered my mother-in-law's phone number, and I called her to contact Chris. I began to cry, which was very unusual for me. I got out of my car and soon found out I had been involved in a three-car pileup. I was the first vehicle. A Pontiac Bonneville traveling about fifty-five miles per hour had rear-ended a Jeep, and the Jeep slammed into me. My cherry-red El Camino was totaled—there was extensive damage to the left rear quarter panel and frame, and the rear window was shattered. My wife came to pick me up, and I had my Camino towed back to the CPC. At least I had another project for the class to work on.

Then I went to the emergency room for x-rays to check for fractured bones. I was fine—no broken bones. Nothing could stop me! I was Frank Antonucci and immune to being hurt—so I thought.

That very next day, Friday, October 9, against my wife's recommendation, I returned to work. I told my students what had happened and how we were going to repair the El Camino. I began my day as I always had in the past, reading the daily memo from the main office. Or, rather, I tried to read it. I couldn't see the print.

A student asked, "What's wrong, Mr. A.?"

I said, "The office must have changed the print on the computer. Bring me my glasses." I still couldn't read it clearly. I wondered what was going on with my eyes. My wife insisted on having me checked for the possibility of a closed-head injury.

I began to cry for no reason. I couldn't remember phone numbers, and when I was driving, I forgot where I was going. Even so, I was still in denial that there was anything wrong with me. I was referred to a neurologist, Dr. Caesar Hidalgo. He did some preliminary testing on me on the following Monday. I hated taking time off from school. What would my class do without me? Dr. H. recommended I see a psychologist, Dr. Jay Inwald, for further testing. My wife drove me to Bingham Farms. Ironically, they could see me that same day (Monday). I never knew how much God played a part in my life. He was with us every step of the way. It is unbelievable how God works and protects us.

We met Dr. Inwald, he gave me some preliminary tests and suggested that I come in for a more extensive series of tests. Chris made the arrangements for the testing, and the scheduler said they could not test me until late December. A person who has a closed-head injury[16] should be treated as quickly as possible. Doing this minimizes the damage done to the brain.

---

[16] Closed-head injuries are a type of traumatic brain injury in which the skull and dura mater remain intact. Closed-head injuries are the leading cause of death in children under four years old and the most common cause of physical disability and cognitive impairment in young people. Overall, closed-head injuries and other forms of mild traumatic brain injury account for about 75 percent of the estimated 1.7 million brain injuries that occur annually in the United States. Brain injuries such as closed-head injuries may result in lifelong physical, cognitive, or psychological impairment and thus are of utmost concern with regard to public health.

The neurological doctor and psychologist worked hand in hand during the healing process. Here is where God came to my rescue. The phone rang, and the scheduler said to my wife, "Excuse me. I have to take this call." A person who had an appointment scheduled for that day was calling to cancel. Could you believe this? Divine intervention. I was still in denial and afraid to be tested.

The scheduler told my wife, "You're in luck. We can test Frank today."

I asked, "Will I need my glasses for the tests?"

Her reply was yes, I would need my glasses. I then informed her I didn't have my glasses and that we would have to come back another day. Chris quickly said, "I will be right back. I am going to the drug store and buy you a pair glasses. We are not going home."

There was no way out of this 8 hour long testing process. I was screwed. As I waited to receive my new glasses, I was taken to a small room where the testing would begin. I was scared out of my mind, but I figured I could bluff my way through this as I had done when I was in high school. I was tested for my cognitive thinking and motor skills. The test consisted of simple written and hands-on problems. I knew I was in trouble when I couldn't assemble blocks or puzzles or solve simple story problems. I was very frustrated and upset with myself.

These tests lasted approximately six to eight hours. I will never forget the words I heard: "It's hard to believe you have two college degrees." I knew at that moment something was wrong with me. However, I thought, "How this can be? After all, everyone is telling me I look fine." I asked myself, "Now what will happen to me? Will I be placed in an institution like Vincent was? Can my brain be repaired? What will everyone think or say? What will my family and students think? Who will support our family?"

On the long quiet drive home, I could hardly talk. My heart was filled with emotion, and I started to cry silently. I didn't want Chris to know I was scared about the future or what was going to happen to us.

I used to hear people say, "This is in God's hands, not yours." I always thought, "Sure. You can't see God, and God is not going to take care of your needs. How can God pay your bills or finish a class project?" The list of things I couldn't do went on and on. What I didn't realize was that God knows and sees everything we do and think. It was time to stop feeling sorry for myself, get my act together and ask God to take charge of my life.

I had two roads to travel: one on the left or one on the right. There was no other alternative. The left was to deny I had a closed-head injury and not proceed with the treatments recommended by the doctors, but just hope for the best. The right road meant get with the treatments and start on the long road to recovery. I knew I had to stop being Mr. Macho Tough Guy. I was forty-eight years old and had a full life ahead of me.

I began group therapy. I immediately thought of Jack Nicolson in the movie *One Flew over the Cuckoo's Nest*. As I sat in group therapy, I listened and silently judged everyone else as they shared how they were feeling. I thought, "Why am I here? I have nothing to share. These people have real problems. I don't have any." Denial. Week after week, I sat there, listened to their stories and what had happened to them. Again, I judged everyone and never looked at myself. I refused to share anything with the group because there was nothing wrong with me. Denial again.

One day, during our group therapy, a female engineer who had a closed-head injury said to me, "Frank, you sit here every week without saying a word to any of us. What is your problem?"

I thought, "Who are you to ask me what my problem is?" I wanted to say I didn't have a problem, but I felt God's presence enter my heart, so I said, "I can't believe this happened to me." The group accepted me for who I was at that moment, not who I had been before my injury. That day was the turning point and the beginning of my recovery.

During the spring, I continued to share my feelings and my fears with the group. We began to bond with one another. I was always doing for others and not wanting others to do for me. I found it difficult to accept help from those who offered it. I always thought I would show weakness by accepting any help. I shared these thoughts with the group one day. I will never forget what they said to me.

"Frank, do you like to give to others?"

I replied, "Yes, all the time. I really like helping others who are in need."

The group asked, "How do you feel when you are giving?"

"I have a great feeling knowing I made a difference in someone's life."

"Frank, why are you preventing those who want to help you also have that great feeling?"

Wow, this hit me like a ton of bricks. I had never thought of the other people. I had only been thinking of myself. I admit I couldn't have made it without the group therapy. I didn't care any longer what people would think of me. I only wanted to get back to work and move on with my life.

As the year progressed, I was learning how to go from point A to point D, bypassing points B and C and masking it. I began to understand and recognize I was not the same man as I was before my accident. I became depressed. My hand-eye coordination was different, and I could no longer tolerate the noises and smells from the body shop. I was too young to retire, and I still had a passion for being with my students. I was too young to be put out to pasture. Also, I was in my twenty-fourth year of teaching, and I needed thirty years in the system to receive a full pension.

In the late spring of 1999, I felt I was ready to return to the classroom. The doctors and human-resources department coordinated a time for my visit to my classroom. I anticipated all kinds of concerns. A substitute was in place, working with my students, and I didn't like anyone invading my space, my domain. I was very territorial and protective of these kids. After all, I knew them best.

My adrenaline rushed as I opened the door of the classroom that I had left eight months earlier. The students were glad to see me and thought I was the same person I always had been before the injury. "It's great to see you, Mr. A. How are you doing? You look fine, Mr. A."

This was a surreal moment, and I couldn't believe I was back but as I looked around, I saw that the classroom was in total confusion. No one could teach it like I had! I wasn't in charge; I was no longer their teacher. This broke my heart.

As the students began to work on their projects, the noise of the grinders and hammers, and the smell of the paint fumes, gave me an instant migraine. Reality set in. I would not be able to return to the body shop. My heart was broken, and I was crying on the inside.

That was my last day in the classroom that I loved so much. I said good-bye to the students who were graduating in June and wished them well. I took one last look around the shop, packed up my personal belongings, and, as they say: "Mr. A. has left the building."

I was deeply hurt that after working there for twenty-four years, after being a loyal, deeply-committed team player and the go-to person in the building, I didn't get a send-off. I was crushed. Throughout my twenty-four years, I had attended and coordinated many fun send-offs for those who were transferred and those who retired. All I had left was my box of stuff and a lot of great memories to hold onto.

The current Auto-Body Shop class at the Career Preparation Center

Life goes on, and time waits for no one. We are all replaceable, but I thought I was the exception. That's a laugh. Have you ever heard these words about our heavenly Father: "He is in control. We are not"? Or maybe "We have been blessed by him"? *I certainly did not think of losing the job I loved as a blessing!*

I thought back to a year before I had my head injury when I got a phone call:

Me: Hello, Auto-Body class. Mr. A. speaking.

Voice: (sounding like a stoner or someone who has been drinking) Do you work on cars?

Me: Yes…

Voice: Can you fix my car?

Me: What do you have?

Voice: A van.

Me: I will have to look at it.

Voice: OK, thank you.

The caller hung up, and I thought, "Man, oh man. Is a student pulling a prank on me or what?"

The next day I arrived as usual, and noticed a beat-up van blocking one of the body-shop doors. I was angry with those who parked and blocked the overhead doors. In the event of an emergency, my first priority was taking care of my students and getting them outside if necessary. The kids began to arrive, and asked, "Hey, Mr. A. Whose piece of junk is parked in front of the door?"

I said I didn't know. A few minutes after the bell rang, the head custodian, Randy, came down and handed me a set of keys. He said someone had dropped a vehicle off early that morning. I said thanks. We moved the van and proceeded with the day's classes. During my late-afternoon class (third session), two men walked through the door. As they approached my desk, I said, "Can I help you?"

I noticed one of the men was very quiet, as if he was intimidated by me. The other had an obviously distorted egg-shaped skull. I didn't say anything, but I couldn't help noticing his head. I introduced myself to the two men, and immediately recognized one of their voices. It was the man I had spoken to on the phone the previous day, but this man was not a stoner and definitely had not been drinking. He gave me his business card. He was from the Macomb County Rehabilitation Department.

As I read the card, I felt as if a golf ball was stuck in my throat. Oh my God, I was so blessed. I immediately thought of Vincent. The other man, the quiet one, asked me if we could repair his van. It was in rough shape and not worth much, very rusty and with a considerable amount of damage. One of my most important guidelines for bringing in a vehicle was that we didn't do rust repair—no exceptions.

The man explained that he wanted to have the van repaired so he could drive it again.

I explained to him that we would be able to repair the collision portion of his van, but we could not address the rusted areas. I asked if this worked for him. He said yes, and thanked me. He also asked how much it would cost. I said I would get back to him the following day with the repair costs.

As the class day ended, we pushed the van into a bay to begin working on it in the morning. The next day, as the seniors arrived, a student named Cal asked me, "What the heck is that piece of junk doing in a stall? I thought we didn't do any rust repair."

I addressed the entire class. "In this world, the roads run north and south, east and west." They appeared puzzled by my analogy. "Life is a two-way street," I clarified. "We give, and we take. Sometimes we give, and we do not receive. This is how life is. It will be easier for you to understand as you get older.

The person who owns this van came to me asking to have it repaired. I am asking you to open up your hearts by helping me to help this man. He is recovering from a closed-head injury. I am not exactly sure what a closed-head injury is, but I know it's not a good thing."

I told the class, "We never know what our future holds for us, what injuries and problems we will face. However, I want your complete support doing this van. This man's van will become a classroom priority, all of the other projects we are currently working on will be placed on hold. What do you think? Are you in or out?"

Cal said, "What are we waiting for? Let's go to work."

I made a few calls and had all the necessary parts donated for the cause. We completed the repair on the van within a few days. I contacted the owner, and the two men came down to pick it up and drive it home. The injured victim asked me how much he owed for the repairs. I told him that my students took care of the repairs, and we had the parts lying around the shop. I went on to say that we wished him a full recovery. "May God bless you," I said.

I received a letter from the rehabilitation center thanking the class for doing an outstanding repair. The letter read, "This was the first time the injured victim had to do something on his own as part of his full recovery."

Who knew that two years later, I would be the one trying to make a full recovery. We think we are in control of everything, but we sometimes forget God is in control of our lives.

My New Assignment

In many ways, I was satisfied with just living day to day. I wanted to continue teaching shop, but I couldn't. I had been good at that and did it well. I once attended a seminar about becoming a change agent, but didn't really comprehend the concept. Now I was a changed man. Gone were the days of being in the shop, having fun with the kids. No more cool cars, no more Autorama, no more working in the shop with the overhead doors open, listening to all the cool tunes.

I planned on doing that until I retired. I didn't want to retire, and I still enjoyed working with students. I wasn't prepared to teach academic classes. I had never worked behind a desk. What could I do now?

I was scared out of my pants. All of the confidence I had gained throughout my years was coming to an end. My teaching certification was vocational and in secondary education, which meant I was qualified to teach in a comprehensive high school. When I attended college, my mentor and good friend Bob had recommended a course of study for me. He told me that with the curriculum he'd suggested, I couldn't go wrong. His advice came to my rescue.

A close friend of mine, Suzy, became the assistant principal at Warren Mott High School. We had previously worked together at the Career Prep Center, where she was a special-needs consultant. There were a number of staff members who were retiring from the district, and a position opened up at Warren Mott High School. Suzy called me and said, "The in-house suspension teacher has retired, and I think this would be an excellent position for you to fill."

She explained that in-house suspension was designed to remove a student who is being disciplined from a classroom, but at the same time allow the suspended student to continue his or her education in a restricted room in the school. Some said it was a jail sentence without bars.

I thought having a suspension classroom within a school was a great idea. Why should the students be rewarded with a day off for not abiding by the school rules?

I jumped at the chance to take this position at Warren Mott. My job was to collect daily assignments from the teachers and consult and counsel the students about why they had been suspended. In the beginning, I had to prove myself all over again. These students didn't know me or my reputation. Once again I had to demonstrate that I was the real deal.

They would not be coming into my classroom for fun and games. If they had discipline problems while with me, I could suspend them from school. Out-of-school suspension could cause them to lose their credits in a class because they weren't able to keep up with their daily assignments. Therefore, I would be holding all the cards.

One day a wise guy came into my classroom and pushed all my wrong buttons. I knew it wasn't going to be a good day for this young man, so I did my best to convince him that I wasn't a normal, everyday, run-of-the-mill teacher. I explained to him that he would not like the consequences he would face if he didn't do his assigned homework. I lost it when he said, "F—K YOU!" especially since his tone was not acceptable.

I reacted like a lion unleashed from its cage. I remembered the day during my first year in the auto-body class when Kevin threatened me because of his failing grade. I came back with a loud and stern voice and said, "You're out of here!"

Staff members came in from adjoining classroom to see if everything was OK. I had forgotten we were in a high school that had paper-thin walls. I told them that everything was under control, and that the student was suspended for two weeks.

This was my favorite part: At the end of his out of school suspension he thought he wouldn't be returning to my classroom and have to complete his originally assigned suspension. I heard a knock on my door and as opened the door here he stood with a sheepish look on his face, almost apologetic. I greeted him with a friendly smile and welcomed him back into my room however he was not happy to see me. Paybacks can be tough but at the end of his term we were on the same page. I reinforced the fact that I was there to help him continue to become successful in school and with expectations of him not to being sent back to me for disciplinary reasons. As the news traveled fast throughout the school, the students had a greater understanding of and respect for me. From that day forward, students who were sent to me knew I was there to help them overcome the reasons they were suspended.

My policy was simple. After a student's suspension was completed, he was welcome to stop by and visit. If there was anything I could help with, I would do so. Being a good teacher requires not only knowledge in the subject matter but patience and understanding. Communication often breaks down between the student and the teacher. I found myself not only helping students to succeed, but I also gave them some strategic suggestions for coping with pressures. What a great feeling that was, being able to make connections with different types of students.

Although it wasn't hands-on, I adjusted well to my new surroundings. I was given time off to attend my group-therapy sessions. I still needed to attend these therapy sessions and to reaffirm my mission in life.

My migraine headaches were strong enough to make me vomit. I was on medication, and when that didn't work, it was change-up time—to a different type of medication. I didn't want to become addicted to such strong medications or become dependent on it. Medication can be a good thing, but when one fails, a new script is written. The new one works for a while and then becomes ineffective, and the beat goes on.

I was in my classroom one day and felt a migraine coming on. I thought, "Holy smokes, what am I going to do?" I went to see Suzy. Her office was right across the hall from my classroom. I said that I needed to go home, that I was not feeling very good.

As I drove north on the freeway, I became more and more nauseated. I couldn't wait to get home. Once home, Chris asked me what was wrong, and I told her my head felt as if a steel band had been wrapped around it. "And it's getting tighter and tighter, like my head is going to explode," I said.

She said, "Have you taken your medications?"

I replied, "No, I don't want any more meds. I have had enough of them!" I lay down on the couch in the den and slept for fourteen hours nonstop. That was the last day I took my meds. I stopped them cold turkey. Was I addicted? I didn't know and didn't want to know. What I knew was that I never wanted to feel that way again. After that day, the headaches lessened, but never completely went away. The doctors said they might continue for the rest of my life? But they were not certain.

I decided to look at the positive side of life. I admired Suzy for becoming an administrator. When she became overloaded, I assisted her with the many student discipline referrals she received from the teachers. I began to think about becoming an administrator. I'd have to give up my summers off and extend my workday.

Suzy was an excellent role model for me to follow. I told her I'd like to move into an administrator's position. She agreed that it was a good idea and would help me grow once again.

The district was offering classes on becoming an administrator. I contacted my old friend Bob, and together we enrolled in the classes.

I began exploring universities that offered a master's degree in administration. I enrolled at Saginaw Valley University in the late summer of 1999. I was very nervous and once again felt uncertain of my future. Last time I took college classes when I was thirty-five. Now I was forty-nine and feeling as if I were starting all over again.

I was once again becoming that guy who was full of determination to beat the odds. However, I also realized that my disability would be a disadvantage for me. My thinking process was slower, and I needed to write everything down. In life, we all have issues, and not everyone really wanted to know—or cared—what had happened to me. I was very guarded about what I said to anyone regarding my disability.

However, I always told my teachers about my accident. My first professor's name was Hanna. She presented the material very clearly and precisely. She explained the course outline in detail, but to be sure I understood, I told her I was a closed-head injury victim and might need additional guidance after class to be sure I was on the right track. She openly accepted me and gave me the confidence I needed.

I felt great driving home after that first class. My classmates were in their mid-thirties or even younger, and I was approaching fifty, so at times, I felt intimidated. However, this was only my perception. I had my many years of teaching experience on my side.

The course met two days a week for six weeks. I adjusted and became more connected with my classmates. Hanna taught the class with passion, and it was fun to learn once again.

I needed thirty credits to obtain my second master's degree, and I was on my way. I had always been a completer, and I never quit. I recalled my army days when we had to stop using the word *can't*. I continued to work full time while I went to school, and once again I had Christine's full and loving support. My days and even the weekends consisted of working, studying and attending school.

In the fall of 2000, I was asked to substitute for an assistant principal at Cousino High School. The administration office said to me this assignment will be for only two or three days, however the two or three days turned out to be eight weeks. I knew this experience will become necessary if I planned on moving into a full time administrative position. The principal's name was Joe, and he ran a tight ship. In fact, he was often referred to as Father Joe.

After we met for the first time, we connected. Our philosophies and visions were very similar. He implemented many old school values there. Cousino was a well-run, disciplined, respected school in the district with that received Blue Ribbon accreditation from the State of Michigan.

I was assigned to East House, with a school population of about eighteen hundred. My duties were as follows: transportation, lunchroom supervision, discipline referrals for the students assigned to my area, supervision of the career-tech programs, evaluations of teaching staff, supervision of after-school events, and whatever else the principal assigned me. My days were long, and I remembered my early days of working as a teacher, when I left my house in the early hours of the morning and returned very late in the evening.

I also was determined to finish my master's degree as quickly as I could. At fifty, I didn't have the stamina I used to have. I enrolled in as many classes as I could to complete my goal. After fifteen months of strong determination, hard work, long hours and a desire to prove to myself that I was again on top of my game, I graduated, earning my master's in administration with a GPA of 3.93 —a solid A average. Not bad for a closed-head-injury victim!

I don't want to mislead you. I might go from point A to point D and skip parts B and C, but I became good at managing my handicap. My two- or three-day substitute position at Cousino turned into eight weeks. I loved it there. Unfortunately, a permanent assistant principal was hired, and I was reassigned to the classroom at Warren Mott High

School. Remember, I used to be a guy who didn't like change.

Now I have a different attitude regarding change. I realized we can become stagnate in our positions. A change of scenery can be invigorating for most. In all walks of life, if we fail to recognize that we have become complacent in our positions, whatever they may be, we can fall into a rut and become unproductive.

Teachers can make or break a student. What we say in the classroom, good or bad, will stay with students for the rest of their lives. I still remembered every detail of that day in my tenth-grade algebra class: "You are too stupid to learn this." We can't erase our negative words from young, impressionable minds.

More Changes in My Future

The 2000 school year was coming to an end. District job postings came out, and I was notified there would be an assistant-principal position opening up. This was an opportunity for me, so I applied. I felt confident, and was ready to begin the next chapter in my career. I seemed to thrive on change at this point in my life.

The human resources office contacted me and scheduled me for an interview. After so many years of teaching, I knew almost everyone in the school district, and everyone knew who Frank Antonucci was. I was liked and respected by many, but there were a few who didn't feel the same. Let's just say I was not on their list of favorites.

Even as I moved into administration, I never lost my vision and continued maintaining my focus and my allegiance to the students for whom I was responsible, by guiding and helping them to develop into responsible adults. I was deeply committed and believed in doing the right thing.

Having my type-A personality was difficult at times, but it worked for me. Every now and then my type-A-ness exploded. However, my two close friends Joe and Suzy suggested strategies to help me keep a lid on, like "Think carefully before you speak" and "Do not say words you may regret." I didn't want my strong personality to work against me, so I used it only to my advantage.

There were times when I was overconfident, and this rubbed people the wrong way. They felt I wasn't approachable and that avoiding me was better than risking a confrontation with me. I needed to remember that my way wasn't the only way. I had to learn to keep an open mind and not to be judgmental before I really listened to what the persons, committees, or groups were saying to me. If I wanted to be a good administrator, I had to become flexible toward all members of our school community and listen to their needs. This included the students, parents, teachers, principals, school-board members, and upper levels of management.

The day of my interview arrived, and I was very confident (but not overconfident) about interviewing for the position of assistant principal. I arrived approximately fifteen minutes before my scheduled time. I wore a dark-blue tailored business suit and tie, and I could see my face in my black shiny shoes. I dressed for success, but I didn't overdo it. I was on a mission to be hired.

I sat patiently and wondered who the interviewers would be and what kinds of questions they would ask of me. Suddenly the door to the interview room opened, and the receptionist said, "Mr. Antonucci, you can come in now." Walking through the door, I was greeted by the superintendent, a human-resources officer, and the associate superintendent. I felt sweat running down from my underarms, and I hoped no one could see that I was nervous. They said, "Come in, Frankie. It's great to see you."

In the beginning, the dialogue was casual—you know, the usual: "How are you doing? How's the family?" Each member of the committee had a notepad and a pen, and they began to ask me questions in a rotating manner. Many different scenarios were presented, and I answered each question slowly and as thoroughly as I could. I was reminded of my mannerisms and style of connecting with the students at all levels.

"Being an administrator requires many long working days that exceed the normal school day's scheduled hours. How do you feel about working beyond the normal scheduled school day?"

I told them, "I do not have any problem working beyond the normal working day. I became aware of the many hours spent beyond the normal school day as I helped my students prepare vehicles for the Autorama. I am not a seven-to-three-thirty person, and my wife supports me every way she can. We have discussed the probability of me working many hours past the regular scheduled day."

"Thank you, Frankie."

I believed they wanted to see if my previous injuries would be a liability for me. They wanted to know how I was feeling, but they did not want to directly address my disability. I knew why they were careful, because of the privacy laws.

The next question was this: "You have been an excellent teacher for many years in the auto-body shop, and you have done things in your classroom that no one but you could ever do. Your reputation and your unique way of motivating those who will not follow the rules is effective, but this committee is concerned with the way you spoke to your students. We are addressing the language that was used in your program. If we decide to move you into an administrator's position, how will you be able to promise the Warren Consolidated School Board that we will not be facing a lawsuit from the parents and community?"

I looked at them square in their eyes and assured them this would not be a problem. "I would never put Warren Consolidated Schools in a situation or jeopardize my position by using inappropriate language—ever." I went on to say that if this occurred, they wouldn't have to fire me. I would resign and not put the district's reputation in a situation that would have a negative effect in the community.

Then the interview chairperson said, "Do you have any further questions for Frankie?" The others shook their heads. He looked at me. "Frankie, do you have any questions for us?"

"Yes. Do you know when the committee will make a decision?"

"Within the next day or two."

I nodded. "I want to thank the committee for giving me this opportunity to apply for this position." As I walked through that door, I saw several more candidates waiting to be grilled by the interview team.

As I drove home, I reflected on the beginning of my career and the unforeseen consequences of my actions. My badass reputation in the classroom could work against me instead of in my favor. Over the years, I had discovered that a good teacher (like a good parent) must be firm and in some cases speak in a language that is relatable and easy to understand. If I were to talk to a group of new teachers about what I learned over the years of being an educator this is what I would tell them:

First of all I would begin to reflect on my classroom days in the body shop. The students I had were hands-on. Don't misunderstand me—they were great kids, but they were the types that needed a shock or two to get motivated.

However here is an explanation of my motivational method. As a new teacher, I'd say to the students at the end of the class period, "OK, everyone. It's clean-up time. Remember to return the tools and the materials to the tool crib, and get ready to go to your next class period."

I was amazed when no one moved. They acted as if I weren't even there. I said to myself, "Maybe they can't hear me." I said again, "It's clean-up time. Everyone return the tools and the materials to the tool crib and get ready to go your next class period."

Same response – no one moved. Then I became uptight. I was the teacher, and I had to be in control. I couldn't and wouldn't let them run over me. If I did, I would lose control of my program. So abruptly, I said in a very loud voice, "OK, you mother f—ers. When I say clean up, I mean clean this f—ing shop up. DO YOU HEAR ME NOW?"

I never saw people move so fast. I remembered how the drill instructors spoke to us in the army—WOW! That was the method I used. If I could have received a college degree in four-letter words, I would have been a scholar.

My foul mouth became an effective teaching tool because it helped me communicate with my students. Maybe this wasn't the "right" way to teach, but that's what happened. I want you, the reader, to understand that the four-letter words I spouted were not directed at them or to them—never in a mean or disparaging way. I loved those kids and respected them too much. I refused to allow anyone to call anyone names, bully, or make fun of anyone. My reputation was very good, and many of the alumni had made successes out of themselves.

I'd say to the class, "I hate to speak like this, using four-letter words to get your attention, but when I speak to you in the appropriate language, I don't have your cooperation. What's going on? This is not appropriate language for a teacher."

They said, "If you spoke any other way, we wouldn't understand you."

Many times, I was described as a drill sergeant or a general. Over the years, I gained the reputation of being an excellent teacher, but people often said, "Too bad he has such a foul mouth."

We never know when our past words or actions may catch up with us. I was grateful to be able to work with those kids who had given up on themselves. Many teachers and principals didn't want my type of students in their classrooms or even in their buildings. The students gifted at academics and sports were golden. They had a place in the vision of a well-run school.

As for my kids, most teachers couldn't communicate with them, and most administrators saw no value in keeping them in their perfect building. Their approach was to suspend and get rid of them. These kids were often referred to as troublemakers. They just needed a strong leader and a role model, someone who genuinely cared for their well-being. In life, what do we expect from the people who have the power to change things for the better? We want strong leaders and great role models. Why should this be any different for our children?

After my interview, I got a phone call from a good friend who was privy to the interview team. He told me their concerns about my capabilities. The district was worried about the potential of being sued because of my habitual use of inappropriate language. I soon received a call to report to the office of the associate superintendent. So I went.

He said, "Come in, Frank, and please close the door. I don't know how to say this, but I want to share with you what's going on with the decision to promote you." He said he believed I would be a good fit within the administration team. However, he was speaking on behalf of the minority.

The interview team was deeply concerned about my inappropriate language, which they commonly referred to as "shop talk." They were asking me again if I would be able to refrain from that type of language, as I would be working with many diverse students. My interactions would be on a much larger scale than what I was used to. My former classroom consisted of approximately 30 students. My assignment in the comprehensive high school would be to cover approximately 450 students.

He asked me, "How will you react when a student you are seeing cusses you out? Will you cuss back?"

I thought, "Wow, is this all they are concerned with?"

I reassured the assistant superintendent that my time working in a hands-on classroom was over, and the foul language was appropriate there, but not in other places. "Thanks for bringing this to my attention. I respect you for telling me this." I told him I was very careful about the type of vocabulary I used and to whom I said it. I made a commitment that I would never embarrass the district or jeopardize my career.

The end of July was nearing, and I still didn't know whether I had made the cut. If I didn't, I'd be back to Warren Mott at my in-house suspension job. If I was promoted, I wouldn't know where I'd be assigned until later in the summer. I also knew the school board had to approve all new positions. Sit and wait. What else could I do?

During the famous Woodward Dream Cruise[17], I ran into the associate superintendent, and he said, "You will be receiving a phone call on Monday. You made the cut." I received another phone call from the administration building asking me to be present at the board-of-education meeting for approval.

---

[17] The Woodward Dream Cruise is the world's largest one-day automotive event, drawing about 1.5 million people and 40,000 classic cars each year from around the globe. Spectators can see muscle cars, street rods, custom, collector and special interest vehicles dating across several decades.

Woodward Dream Cruise
By Stephen K. Donnelly at en.wikipedia [Public domain]

Within the a few days, I received a letter from Cousino High School. It read, "Welcome to Cousino! We are pleased to have you join our team. Respectfully, Joseph Sayers." My wife and I were very happy and proud. I thought, "Here I am—a C student and a hands-on person—and now I am the assistant principal at a Blue Ribbon high school."

Labor Day weekend was coming up, soon school would be in full swing and students would be in the halls, excited to meet their new teachers. I couldn't wait until the first day to see the staff and my secretary once again.

On my first day, Joe welcomed me aboard and gave me a list of my duties and responsibilities. He also said, "I want to know the pulse of my building."

I said, "No problem. You will be in the loop, and thank you for choosing me to return to Cousino." The staff gave me a warm welcome and were glad to see me. I immediately reconnected with everyone. As I walked through the halls of this huge high school, the students who had been in the ninth and tenth grades when I was last there were now juniors and seniors. They recognized me and welcomed me back.

"It's great to see you, Mr. A."

"Hey, Mr. A. How's it going?"

"Mr. A., are you back for good this time?"

My replies were, "Thank you, yes, and I am happy to return as your assistant principal."

I was on a mission to reconnect with the students and staff. I wanted them to see me as approachable. I knew some weren't in favor of me returning. However, to be an assistant principal, you have to have thick skin. I wasn't assigned to be a contestant in a personality contest; I was there for the betterment of the students and staff.

Joe, also known as Father Sayers, continued to maintain a school atmosphere that was safe, moral, and, most of all, well disciplined. Cousino set the bar high and was a tough act to follow. The principal of any high school makes all of the decisions that set the tone and determines how the students and staff will buy in. Joe set the tone for Cousino.

My office was located in West House, and I was assigned to approximately six hundred students. The total number of students enrolled in the school was approximately eighteen hundred, and the student body was divided into three groups alphabetized by last name. My day began at 6:30 a.m., and could end at 5:00 p.m., 6:00 p.m., or even 7:00 p.m. I had many duties; the main one was to ensure that the school environment was a safe place in which students could learn, grow up, understand and know the consequences of not following the guidelines of the student code of conduct.

One of my responsibilities was to enforce and maintain that student code of conduct—in other words, school discipline. I was fair, but I wouldn't let anyone run over me or think I was a pushover. These kids ranged in age from fourteen and a half to eighteen years of age. If a student had a problem, the teacher would write a referral and send that to my office along with the student. The student and I would discuss it, and I listened to his or her side of the problem. The teacher's referrals were valid, because the teachers wanted to maintain integrity in their classrooms as I did back in the days of my auto-body program. Once in a while, I would receive a teacher's referral that was frivolous or absurd. I would still address the teacher's concern and discuss it with the student. Then I'd send the student back to class.

Here's an example of one such referral. It read, "I want this student removed from my class. She didn't have a pencil today." Deep down inside, I said to myself, "Teacher, are you kidding me? You sent this student down to see me because she didn't have a pencil?" But when I talked to the student, I said, "The next time you need a pencil, stop by my office, and we will give you a pencil. I do not want to see you back in this office for any disciplinary action. Do I make myself clear?"

"Yes, Mr. A."

I ended, as I always did, by saying in a nonthreatening manner, "Have a great day and learn as much as you can today."

Many of these students only needed the fear of God put into them, but others needed to be punitively disciplined for their actions. There were times I would have to expel students for violating the student code of conduct for serious things like drugs, fighting, assault, or harassment. The word soon got out, and I became known for taking care of business in a just manner without favoritism.

I stood in the hallways on a daily basis, reminding students that the first bell had gone off, and they needed to get to class quickly or they would be sent to my office for being tardy.

I wore many hats: counselor, referee, disciplinarian, transportation coordinator, parking-lot attendant, and security guard. In addition to my student responsibilities, I was assigned to write teacher evaluations and evaluate the curriculum for the vocational-education programs within our building. My plate was loaded, but I loved what I was doing. I was making a difference within the walls of Cousino and continuing to support us in our status as a Blue Ribbon high school at both the state and national levels.

In early spring, the seniors were excited to share their acceptance letters from major colleges and universities throughout the country. As they filled out the line that asked them the name of the high school they had last attended, they were proud and eager to write "Cousino High School." These three words were golden on an application and gave them the leading edge over other applicants. I reflected on my days at Lakeview High School. Was that all I wanted? To graduate and get out of there? Nothing more, nothing less? I had rarely participated in any after-school activities or functions. Making money and working on my car were the top of my priority list.

Even then, deep down inside, I missed the after-school activities and sporting events. I often regretted missing out on the fun of being in high school. Like the 1986 movie with Rodney Dangerfield named *Back to School*, when he returns to high school – that was me. When I returned to the halls of high school, I felt I had been given a second chance to enjoy those activities. However, this time around, I was the adult who was responsible for the student body. Coordinating schedules and supervising these events with the staff was another part of my weekly schedule, and I loved doing this.

Tuesday, September 11, 2001

On one September day of my first year as an assistant principal, I was busy with my responsibilities—walking the halls and making sure everyone was in the right classroom. The sun was shining, and it was a beautiful fall day.

Suddenly a senior saw me and came running out of the cafeteria. "Hey, Mr. A. Did you hear what happened in New York, DC and Pennsylvania?"

I said, "No, I didn't. What happened?"

"Come into the cafeteria and see for yourself."

I couldn't believe what I was seeing. I stood there mute, and my eyes began to water. Our country was under attack. Oh my God! I soon received a call on my two-way radio from the principal: "Mr. A., report to the office."

We were briefed as the phones rang off the wall. All the parents were panicking for the safety of their children. Luckily, the principal was experienced in these types of emergency situations, and I followed his commands to the letter. With a population of eighteen hundred students and the parents coming to pull their children out of school, if there hadn't been a procedure in place, there would have been mass hysteria and chaos. The safety of the students and parents was first and foremost. We had to keep focused and stay calm.

After the students were dismissed and the premises vacated, the principal had a staff meeting and briefed all of us about the day's events. The staff was dismissed, and the atmosphere in the building was quiet and solemn. A few of the staff members had relatives and children working in the area of the terrorist attacks. That evening, all after-school activities were canceled.

It was a day to remember!

The Cousino Parking Lot

I loved being the assistant principal in a Blue Ribbon high school. My responsibilities included evaluating the teaching staff, supervising the lunchroom, student discipline, coordinating parent teacher conferences, supervising after school athletic events naming just a few. However my least favorite was traffic control and the student parking lot!

The parking lot had many problems, not enough spaces for the amount of students who drover their cars to school. We couldn't accommodate everyone, therefore the seniors were given priority. Parking permits were distributed prior to the beginning of the new school year for all seniors who had met the requirements: proof of a valid driver's license, proof of insurance, and a valid vehicle registration. Upon receiving their permit, students were required to sign and follow the list of dos and don'ts. Our security team patrolled the parking lots to be sure everyone was parked legally and displayed their permit clearly in the window. Those who drove cars and parked them in the lot without a permit were given warning stickers and logged into the security guard's report, which was submitted to me at the end of each school day.

One student in particular received multiple warnings from me. I reminded him on a weekly basis that he must purchase a parking permit, or there would be severe and costly consequences. Time and time again, he said, "Yes, Mr. A. I will, Mr. A. OK, Mr. A." I even offered to give this student a parking pass in weekly installment payments of three dollars per week, but he wanted to beat the system and not conform to the school rules. I told him I was finished playing his games and trying to accommodate him.

One of our more popular programs in our high school is a student-operated combined radio/television program. The students would stop by my office on a regular basis looking for a story to tape for the daily announcements. These stories would be viewed by the student body at the end of fourth hour. I contacted the teacher and said, "Today, I will have a story for your students to video. Have your camera crew meet in my office at nine thirty this morning." I then called security. "Security, do we have that same red car parked in the lot again? The one without a parking permit?"

"I will take a look, Mr. A. Yes, it's out here."

"Please confirm there isn't a parking permit placed in the windshield."

"Confirmed, Mr. A."

I made a phone call to the local towing and flatbed company and told them that we had a vehicle in our parking lot that would need to be removed immediately. The dispatcher said, "Make and model please. And who am I speaking to?"

"This is Frank Antonucci, assistant principal at Cousino High.. When can you get here and remove it?"

"We will be there in fifteen minutes."

"Great. I will meet you in the parking lot."

By that time, the camera crew was in my office. I said, "Let's go." I took the microphone, and the cameras were rolling. I began to address the student body. "Good morning, everyone. Time and time again, we have stressed the importance of maintaining a safe and secure parking lot for everyone to use.

"Many of you have followed the rules by purchasing a parking permit, and in the event that you did not, you were given an opportunity to purchase a permit. This morning you are witnessing a case where a student who has been given multiple warnings and opportunities to comply, has failed to do so.

"Therefore, by the time this story is broadcast during fourth hour, your vehicle will have been removed from the parking lot and taken to a storage yard. Please be sure to see me before the end of the school day, and I will give you the location and the cost of picking up your vehicle. I hope this will clearly send a message to those of you who continue to park illegally in our school lot. Thank you, and enjoy the rest of the school day."

I was the talk of the school that day. We sold at least five more parking permits.

My secretary said to me, "There is a young man here to see you."

"Who is it?"

"The student whose car was impounded this morning."

"Send him in." When the boy walked in, I said, "Sit down. What can I do for you today?"

"I can't believe you had my car impounded!"

"Believe it. I gave you ample warnings and opportunities to do the right thing, and now you will have to pay $150 to get your car out of the impound lot. Life can be good if you take the advice of those people who want to help you. However, the learning curve can be costly. Here is the location of your vehicle and the phone number. I will have it towed again if I see it in the parking lot without the proper parking permit. Do I make myself clear?"

This message quickly ran through the student body as if I had poured gasoline on a fire.

Football

Although I worked many long hours, I enjoyed the Friday-night home football games. All of the administrators were on duty, supervising the students who were in attendance. During these events, the students had the flexibility to have fun, make some noise, and cheer for their favorite team.

Our duties were to take care of any situation that occurred and to ensure the safety of everyone enjoying the game. The parent booster club sold food, refreshments, and fifty-fifty raffle tickets. This was a great time to meet and become actively involved in the community.

Our principal had been a quarterback at a major university, and he was still an avid sports-minded person. He was well versed in all of the major sporting teams, scores, and stats. One night after the football game, we went onto the football field, and he carried a football in his hands. He said, "Go out, and I will throw a pass."

I choked up and thought, "Go out for a pass? Is this guy nuts?" Aloud, I said, "Joe, this is the first time I have been on a football field in my life. I have never caught a football either."

He said, "Are you kidding me?"

"No, I was a car guy and not very coordinated and didn't have the confidence to play any type of sport."

I remember him saying, "Oh my God." He began to show me how to catch a football and throw one too. I ran across the lighted vacant field as he threw me the ball, and I miraculously caught his pass. I will never forget that day with Joe at Cousino High School.

Another Assignment

Later that year, the rumor mill began to suggest that the administrators were going to be offered a buyout from the district as an incentive to retire. I didn't pay too much attention to rumors. Every day, there would be something else or someone saying something different. I wanted to stay focused on my job and not the rumor.

However, I soon discovered that the rumors of the state encouraging early retirement were true, and the district was offering monetary incentives to that end. If a number of building principals were about to retire, I realized that there would be a number of principal positions that will need to be filled—including at Cousino, since Joe planned to retire. I began to fantasize about becoming a building principal. Wow! First, a teacher, an assistant principal and then a principal—how cool would that be?

I had mixed feeling about moving up the ladder. I really enjoyed working at Cousino, and Joe was a good leader and mentor to me. I recalled how my good friend Suzy set the example for me to follow and gave me the encouragement and confidence to move forward, to advance myself within the school system. I reflected back to the days when she said to me as I was beginning my internship, "If you want to be an administrator, you better not laugh in the meetings." Could I *really* become the next principal of Cousino High School?

As word got out that the district would have to fill Joe's shoes, a few members of the student booster club came to my office and said, "We are signing petitions in and around the community for you to become the next principal here at Cousino." I choked up when I heard the news, but the booster club didn't decide who would become the next principal. The school board was in control and would make their recommendation to the superintendent of the district. The school board was a very powerful group of people from the community, and some had large egos too.

Joe had made Cousino High School a national Blue Ribbon school and an excellent example for all schools to follow. His personality was strong for the right reasons, and he got the job done, with or without the approval of the board of education. Those with large egos didn't like Joe's methods of getting it done first and asking permission later. My style of getting a job done was a carbon copy of Joe's.

There were seven members on the board, and the politicking began. One day, I received a phone call from the superintendent saying, "Frankie, meet me in my office today at three."

I drove over to the administration office thinking, "What is he going to say to me?" I arrived, and his secretary announced my presence. "He is ready to see you. Go on in."

I shook his hand as he said, "Please sit down. You have done a great job at Cousino, and the parents and students love you. They love you so much they are signing petitions to have you become the next principal over there. But I am getting pressure from a few members of the board *not* to assign you to Cousino.

"Therefore, I am assigning you to become the next district director of career technical education and the principal at the Career Preparation Center—and that is what will happen. Furthermore, I don't want a f—ing word about this meeting said to anyone. Do you understand, Frankie?"

"Yes, and thank you for the promotion. I will not share this with anyone."

The superintendent had caved to the board members in order to save his own behind. I didn't care where I would be reassigned. However, I would have enjoyed continuing the vision and tradition of our former principal at Cousino and to continue my rapport with the students and staff I had worked with.

The 2004-2005 school year was ending, and I was about to begin a new chapter of my life. I had overcome many challenges, and was about to begin the next stage of a journey that I had never imagined as a kid that I'd take.

In August of 2005, I would be back at the school where I began my career as a teacher in 1975. I would be the principal of the building and the director for career and technical education—a big title with many responsibilities. I thought about how far I'd come from my early days in elementary school through my negative and embarrassing experiences in my high-school algebra class. I was a fighter, and I was out to prove that those who worked with their hands shouldn't and couldn't be written off as "those kids." It was now time for everyone to see what "those kids" were worth. I would be their advocate and promoter. The proverbial ball was in my court. Let the games begin!

Principal and Director: The Final Chapter

In August, 2005, I said good-bye to the staff at Cousino and received many cards congratulating me on my promotion. I was overwhelmed by the send-off gifts and compliments. This was not the good-bye I had when I had to leave Career Prep Center as a teacher.

Many were disappointed that I would not be staying at Cousino High School. They asked, "Why are you leaving us?" and "We love you here. Why can't you stay?" and "We signed petitions. What happened?"

I told them, "As you know, my expertise is in career technical education, and the district needed someone just like me to fill the shoes of a director who retired."

I didn't dare tell them the truth. The conversation I had with the superintendent was never to be shared—ever. I thanked them for all of the gifts, cards and kind words and returned to my office to pack my personal belongings, including the football Joe had signed and given to me. My secretary had tears in her eyes and gave me a hug and said, "I will miss you, Mr. A. Please keep in touch, and don't become a stranger. Come back and see us!"

I loaded up my car and drove north to my new assignment. When I arrived, the current principal (soon to be former) was finishing up his work to close out the current school year. He would show me the procedures and walk me through the protocol. I had known him for many years because I was a teacher who worked under his direction when he was an assistant principal. He had been my boss.

Home Again

It was September, 2005. I walked through the front door of the building, the secretarial staff greeted me. They knew me from my days as a teacher, and it was great to be in a position to work with a familiar administration staff. The principal's office had not yet been vacated, so I placed my personal belongings in the counselor's office.

The soon-to-be-retired principal had an ego as big and as wide as a barn door. I received a lukewarm welcome from him. "Hello, Frank."

I could see and feel his attitude. However, I said to him with a smile as big as the Golden Gate Bridge, "Hello. I am grateful to be here, and I hope I can fill your large shoes."

Sometime we all have to step up to the plate and become humble. After all, he was only days away from retiring, and I didn't really care what he was thinking. My sole purpose for moving up the ladder was to help "those kids." He eventually gave me a crash course on the pulse of the building. He looked as thrilled to do so as if I were looking into his wallet or rifling through his personal business. He was very territorial. He wasn't about to teach me the ropes or give me the ins and outs of his building.

His last big day came, and we said good-bye to the retiring principal. I said to myself, "Good-bye, you territorial prick. Don't let the door hit you in the behind!"

I moved my personal belongings into MY office and began to organize and become familiar with the few files that had been left behind. I'd taken a big step to move here and felt overwhelmed. I sat and said to myself, "The buck stops here with me. I am responsible for all that will take place in my building. I am now the go-to person."

When I thought back on my final days at the CPC in June 1999, there hadn't even been a card, send-off—nothing. I felt bitter then, and still had that bitterness inside of me. Actually, I was more hurt than angry.

Many of the teaching staff who had been my colleagues were still teaching at the school, and now I was their boss. I would be evaluating them and listening to their issues. So, I could no longer be their friend. I was their principal. I couldn't show any type of favoritism, and I definitely could not reflect how I felt about my send-off. Although they had been working there when I left, I had to bury my feelings and become a strong leader and a good role model for them as well as the newly-hired staff.

We all have some kind of baggage or a past we do not want to return to. Mine was my inappropriate use of the English language in the body shop. After all, I never once thought I would become the principal or be working with my own staff. I had to watch my language now and be careful of what I said and did. You never know when your past behavior will be staring you in the face.

I couldn't change what I had said or done throughout my years. I always believed in being honest. I could only learn from my mistakes and move on. I will be judged by God when I meet him, and he will look at what I have done with my life and how I used the talents he gave me.

The school year was about to begin. The staff would be coming in to prepare their classrooms and lessons for the incoming students. This was the time for our first staff meeting and for me to hand out the necessary supplies and emergency card information. It was also time to meet and introduce the staff members. As principal, I had to deliver a message sharing the district's vision for the school year.

I was very nervous. This was my first time in charge of a staff meeting, and I wanted to sound sincere and approachable to all new and veteran staff members. I introduced myself and welcomed everyone back for the new school year. I also introduced my assistant principal, as she was new to the district. I told the staff how excited I was to return to the school where I began my teaching career in 1975 and shared my teaching experiences with them.

Then, I told them: "I want to be open and transparent with you from the very first day we are working together. Because I, too, was a teacher, I still consider myself to be a teacher first and an administrator second. I understand your jobs; we are alike in that.

"As a teacher, I remembered how we listened to the principal speak, then we'd retreat to the staff lounge and talk about him. I know some of you will ask the veterans who I am and how I will be to work for. Some will tell you stories of my colorful past. Others will not say too much. Well, this morning I'll share with you who I am, who I was and how I got here—so you can hear it from the source.

"I will begin. I taught auto-body repair for twenty-four uninterrupted years until I had the misfortune to be in a life-changing automobile accident. Because of my injuries I could not work in the auto shop any longer. I worked at Warren Mott, assigned to deal with students in the in-house suspension room. While there, I became interested in becoming an administrator, and enrolled in college to earn my second master's degree in administration. I was assigned to Cousino High School as assistant principal and loved it. That opportunity gave me a chance to see the inner workings of a comprehensive high school, a much-needed experience. I began to learn the process the counselors used to schedule students who wanted to attend our school. Understanding this process will be vital to increase our student population. The school district continuously reviews the amount of student attending in all its buildings.

"I also want to tell you about my personal attributes and challenges. Yes, it's true; I had a foul mouth and was also reprimanded for not following the protocol of the principal. I broke the rules on behalf of my students. Auto shop hands-on students were looked down upon, but they were my first priority. I had minimal and confrontational support from the administration team at that time. I wanted to turn left, and they wanted me to turn right. I could never meet my student's needs and satisfy the unachievable demands of the administration. Therefore, I did things my way and what I felt was best for my students.

"In closing, I want you to know that I will not be confrontational, and I will be more than willing to facilitate you and your students in any way that I can.

I will also tell you we are working in a different climate now, and I cannot permit the use of inappropriate language. If you have difficulties with this, please see me in my office, and we can discuss a few strategies that may work for you. I am here to help you reach maximum success with all of your students. Have a great school year, and welcome back."

The staff stood up, applauded me and congratulated me as their new principal and director.

The Students Meet Us

It was exactly thirty years after I began my first day of teaching auto-body in the classroom. Today I would be meeting the students as their principal. What a great feeling of accomplishment this was for me and my family.

As I drove to the school on the freeway with my air conditioning turned on high, I looked forward to seeing the students arrive. Although the fall season was around the corner, the Michigan summer humidity was thick in the air, and I didn't want to get out of my car all sweaty in appearance, my hair dripping wet from sweat and messed up. Throughout my years, I had seen administrators who looked sloppy and didn't care what they looked like—as if they never looked in the mirror. To me, appearance was still first and foremost. As building principal, I would set the tone of the building. I had told my staff, "How can you earn your students' respect if you dress like a slob? If you're going to grow a beard, please trim it and be professional about it. Ladies, please dress professionally."

Every morning, before I walked out the door, I put on a dark business suit, a dress shirt with a button-down collar, one of the many cool-looking ties my loving wife, Christine, had purchased for me, and highly polished black shoes. If I had facial hair, it was neatly trimmed and with razor-sharp lines. My wife, the inspector, gave me the once-over, similar to the inspections my drill sergeant in the army gave me.

"Good morning," Chris would say and give me a kiss on the lips. "Have a great day, and good luck." Then she'd look at me again. "Please change that tie. It doesn't match the color of your shirt."

234

"What? I like it."

"OK, it's your tie. Dress the way you want to dress. I am not going to say anything to you anymore."

I'd go back to my closet and pick out another tie to match my shirt. Then I went back into the kitchen and waited for my sergeant to approve. "How do I look?" Chris knew I was very conscientious about my appearance, and she was my best critic.

"Much better."

We'd kiss good-bye and she'd say, "Be safe and have a great day. I love you."

On this first day of school, I pulled into the principal's parking spot—*my parking spot now*! I couldn't wait to go into my office and log into my computer to be ready for my first day of school and the arrival of our students. As the staff entered the building, many stopped by my office and said, "Good morning, Mr. A. Great to have you as our principal, Mr. A. We are excited to be here this year, Mr. A." Receiving their affirmation gave me the confidence to know I could succeed.

Not all of the staff were excited and happy to see me. Some staff members I had worked with throughout the years were slugs—only there for their paycheck. They wanted to do as little as possible for their students. I knew this, and they knew I was onto their foolish games.

Teaching is not much different than other types of jobs. Some staff worked for the betterment of the students, but we also had proverbial whiners and complainers too. As the building union representative for a number of years, I had been the mediator between staff members and the principal on more than one occasion. Therefore, I knew more than I cared to know. These staff members were still employed by the district and were not on my welcoming committee as the word got out I would be returning as their principal. They felt threatened, and knew that the party might soon to be over for them.

I knew a few strategies that I could use with these staff members. I had to be careful and keep my opinions and observations to myself without being prejudiced or biased. Everyone deserves a fair shake, and maybe these teachers would wake up and see that their mission was actually as high school teachers and good role models.

Before the students arrived, I made an announcement on the PA. "Will all staff report to the cafeteria for a brief staff meeting."

They all walked in, sat down, and I started. "Good morning, everyone. Today is an opportunity for everyone to make a difference and develop positive rapport with the students. Remember, be friendly and welcome them into your classrooms. Be sure to give them an outline with your classroom expectations clearly stated in language that is easy for them to read. Remember to be firm and win them over. Most of all, do not give the farm away. You are in control of the students and in control of your success. Best of luck. I will be walking throughout the building to set the tone, and give the students an opportunity to meet their new principal."

The phrase "giving away the farm" meant not having any firm disciplinary consequences in a classroom or employing a grading system that would not be a challenge for the students. Early on, I had found that the students had the grading system figured out and knew how to use it to their advantage. If a teacher did not hold on to the integrity of their classroom during the first ten weeks of school, they would not have classroom control in the thirtieth week of school. I coached my staff using the lessons I'd learned from experience in my early years.

I continued. "Do not berate your students, and do not tell or teach them something you cannot support. These kids are much more astute than you may believe. Don't underestimate these kids.

"I watched the students arrive this morning, and I observed that only about half were dressed appropriately for attending our school. The other half were not. I ask you to support me in reinforcing a moderate school dress code. I will address this when the appropriate time comes."

I wasn't about to place any more rules, requests, or forms on the teachers then. "Take it nice and slow," I reminded myself. "Rome wasn't built in a day." I dismissed the teachers to their classrooms. And school began for the day.

Before I knew it, the first day of school and my first day as principal was over. The dismissal bell rang out loudly and I watched the students make a mad dash for the buses and their cars. I walked outside to be sure everyone left the school grounds in a reasonably safe manner. I watched the students and the staff, and considered how I could make our school more user friendly.

Once again, I made the announcement, "All staff members report to the cafeteria." When they were gathered, I asked, "Well, how did it go today?"

Most were excited to see and meet their new and returning students. However, some were already counting down the days until Christmas vacation. I knew who they were, and asked, "Do you have any questions or concerns for me? I want to help you get the school year off to a great start."

"Mr. A.," one veteran staff member asked, "When will the parents become responsible for their children? Why do we have to discipline them? I believe it is not the teacher's job to be the parent. I am tired of doing this. The good kids are not the problem. It's the ones who will not follow the rules."

I had to keep my cool. I was the principal and speaking in front of a professional staff, addressing a staff member who had fewer students than most of the other staff members in the building. That teacher had a total of twenty-six students, while everyone else had fifty to seventy students. I was uptight about addressing this staff member's question, but it was the time to show everyone I wasn't the same Frank Antonucci they once knew.

I said this: "I understand today's students have become more and more challenging. However, I will give everyone a snapshot of them. Let's take a look at the typical American household. Mom and Dad are both working to support their families, with many financial responsibilities, just as we all have in our own personal lives.

"A typical morning might look like this. Everyone is up at six thirty. Mom and Dad are getting ready for work. The kids are scrambling and being reminded to get their butts in gear before they miss the bus. Sometimes, the kids eat breakfast, but many don't have the time to eat anything before they get to school. Many barely made it to the bus on time. They come into our classrooms hungry and poorly dressed. At the end of the school day, they get back onto the bus and head for home.

"These kids sometimes return to empty houses without any adult supervision. Mom and Dad return from their stressed-filled workdays and are tired from the day as well. Maybe Mom makes dinner, or maybe they will be eating something from a carry-out restaurant or fast-food place. Not much dialogue goes on between the kids and their parents. As the day comes to a close, everyone will go to bed, only to awake and repeat the day once again.

"We are the first people they see and make contact with. We are the ones they will seek out and talk to. We are the ones who will notice if they are in need or hungry or abused. I hope this answers the question for you and the rest of our staff."

With a smile on my face, I said, "Great question. Thank you for bringing this to my attention." Most were nodding their heads in agreement, but there were those who didn't agree with me. That was OK. I was there to be a good leader and not necessarily win a personality contest.

I also wanted to set the tone for my staff. I would not tolerate a staff who were there for their own agenda. I wanted to share what I had learned in my classroom and dealing with kids during my thirty years with the district. I had witnessed and experienced firsthand those students who had slipped through the system. I didn't want to repeat this in my building. I wanted to avoid social promotion. I knew I would be held accountable for the successes and failures of the building. I was blessed that I learned how to develop strategic goals so I could support the vision of this talented and experienced staff.

In the weeks to come, I worked to adjust the building atmosphere and environment for everyone. Walking around the building, popping in and out of the classrooms were my regular habit. Being visible is a key factor for being a successful principal. I wanted to observe the students' behavior in the classrooms, halls, and parking lot. In the mornings, my presence was visible as I stood in the main entrance of the building greeting the students as they entered the building.

"Good morning, Mr. A."

"Good morning, Jim. How are you doing? Do you know what day it is?"

"No."

"Today is free Tuesday."

Jim gave me a blank stare and said, "Free Tuesday?"

"Yes. You can learn as much as you want to learn today."

"Oh, Mr. A. You're too funny," he said with a smile on his face, as he walked to his classroom. I wanted the students to know I had a sense of humor, and they were there to learn and have fun. Those who needed an adjustment in their behavior knew I was *not* the person they wanted to see.

We had close to six hundred students enrolled in our building, and the administration and school board continuously placed the CPC on the chopping block in an attempt to close it. Their goal in the district was to reduce operating costs and spread the savings throughout the district. The staff and I all knew if we didn't become unified and increase our student enrollment, we would be doomed. Many of the programs and curriculums needed to be overhauled and modified to meet current trends and industry requirements.

Schools like ours offered career and technical education necessary to keep our society going. We offered vocation training for young men and woman to prepare them for work in health services, auto repair and maintenance, printing, commercial arts and many other areas of expertise.

Update Time

The building's physical structure and appearance, inside and outside, had not been updated in the past thirty years. I saw the students who arrived early in the mornings sitting on the floors in the hallway with their classmates, reviewing for tests, and exchanging notes from their notebooks. This disturbed me, and I asked myself "Why do these kids have to sit on the floor? Why isn't there an area—maybe a student commons area—where they can sit? This is ridiculous. I will change this immediately. Today will be the last day they will be sitting on the floor."

I said to my secretary, "I will be right back. If you need something, call me on my cell phone." I hopped in my pickup truck, drove to the local hardware depot and purchased ten decorative park benches. I planned to place them in the halls and foyer by the main entrance. As I drove back to the school, I called my secretary and said, "Have the custodian meet me at the receiving area. I am pulling into the parking lot."

"Good morning," the custodian said.

"Let's unload the truck," I said, "and then I want you to go down to the building trades program and ask the teacher if you can have a few students to help you assemble these park benches. I want this done immediately. When our students walk into the building tomorrow, I want them to have a place

241

to sit down—from tomorrow on, I do not want to see any students sitting on the floor again. Do I make myself clear?"

"Yes, Mr. A. I often wondered why these kids had to sit on the floor and why the district didn't provide a place for them to sit."

"Great question. The district didn't, but I will. It is the principal's responsibility to provide a conducive and safe learning environment for all students."

I walked into the building the following day at 6:30 a.m. and was very pleased to see the benches strategically placed in the halls and in the foyer. They looked great. At 6:55 a.m., the students started to arrive. The expressions on their faces were priceless as they saw the benches. I'm sure they were thinking, "Why are they here? Who put them here? Can we sit on them?"

Someone finally asked me "Excuse me, Mr. A. Can we sit on the benches?"

"Of course! These benches are for you kids to use and enjoy. Please feel free to sit on them. I never want to see you guys on the floor again."

"Thank you, Mr. A.!"

As the staff walked in and saw my first improvement, they were almost speechless. I heard "It's about time we did something for these kids."

I thought, "Why didn't the building policy committee bring this issue to the former building principal's attention?"

More small changes took place. My passion for career technical education was at an all-time high. I'd say to anyone who would listen, "Why don't we have this for the students? Why can't we do that for our kids? We can create a school climate that will make the kids want to attend. Doing small things will increase student enrollment and show the district we are actively pursuing a dream of more students enrolled in our programs."

I firmly believed that a school should be operated with a tough discipline policy. This, I believed, would send a message to the parents, students, and the community that the CPC was an excellent school to attend. As I began to observe those students who had behavior problems, I couldn't believe what I was witnessing. They walked the halls without permission from a teacher, gambled on a teacher's computer, played cards in the classroom, walked down the halls as if they were in the movie *Blackboard Jungle*, smoked in the bathroom, carried around open soft drinks spiked with alcohol, brought cocaine into the building, sat all over the main office furniture and were disrespectful to the secretarial staff.

These were the students who had attended the CPC under the supervision of the previous administration, so they were used to getting away with this type of behavior. I am not suggesting that the previous building principal didn't care or have discipline procedures in place. I understood that enforcing the district's disciplinary policies and enforcing progressive discipline procedures is very time consuming. It could bury an administrator, preventing them from completing the many other responsibilities of a building principal.

When I was an assistant principal at a countywide in-service meeting, a fellow administrator asked me, "How is the discipline in your high school?"

My response was this: "All I do is suspend students, and at times, it is stressful dealing with the fallout from the parents and the students who are being suspended. Most of the parents are sure their child has done nothing wrong."

I discussed what I'd said with the principal to whom I was currently assigned, and he said, "How many students do you see on a regular basis?"

I said, "Approximately 130. I'm not sure. However, some are continuous repeat offenders."

"That's less than 10 percent of the student body here. Try to look at the positive students, not the negative."

I had never looked at it that way. His insight gave me a new perspective. My attitude changed quickly and I became more positive. The students who knew me from the years walking the halls of Cousino knew they didn't want to be on my wrong side. There was a new sheriff in town, and it was now time to clean up Dodge City. The fear of God was coming down on those who wanted to run the school their way.

My assistant principal was new to the position and had never had to discipline students. His role as my assistant meant wearing many hats and dealing with issues, such as warning students, giving detentions, developing strategies for changing student behavior, suspending or expelling students, all while developing a rapport with the community.

The goals we set for ourselves were high, and if we were going to raise student enrollment, we had to dig deep and work hard. The Career Preparation Center's reputation was often referred to as "a place for *those* kids."

It was also referred to as a retirement home for teachers because the total student enrollment was approximately six hundred, about sixteen hundred less than the comprehensive high schools. My mission was to raise student enrollment and shed our retirement-home reputation. The students and parents needed to see that this administration would not tolerate students who did not follow the program of this school.

The staff and students would now see the other side of Frank Antonucci. Goliath was now awake. Hang on to your seats! I intended to transform our school into one of Michigan's best career and technical education centers. I wanted us to be called "a place that kids are fortunate to attend." A school filled with dignity, pride and school spirit.

The Team

Being a change agent can be a good thing. That happens if the changes are subtle and the stakeholders have a positive attitude. I knew I wasn't working in a utopia, but I am an optimistic person. I see the glass as half full. I realized that change for some could be very difficult. After all, there had been a time in my life when I was very resistant to change, when I didn't want my space and comfort disrupted, when I didn't want to change anything. I decided to devise a plan that would be in the best interests of the students, community, and staff.

I prioritized the needs of the building. First on the list was to develop and enforce the school district's student code of conduct. The teachers had to believe they had the support they needed from the new administration team. Their participation would be necessary, since they wrote student misconduct referrals for any infraction of the rules. We were going to come down very hard on those students who interfered and disrupted my plan for a fun, safe and productive learning environment. I asked the security guard to assist me by being visible in the halls, parking lot, and lavatories.

The climate of the school culture began to change as the students received consequences for their negative actions. The word spread out through the student body and reached those who were regularly truant and tardy for their classes. Slowly we saw a reduction in the number of students who lingered in the hallways and the parking lot as the tardy bell rang.

The staff could also see that the school was going through a positive transformation and was on the road to becoming a premier school. I often reminded them, "If we become tough and fair, the community will take note and the student enrollment will increase. Let's make our school a commodity for all to observe."

On our mandated end-of-year report for the district, we reported that there were 120 students temporally suspended for infractions of the student code of conduct and that we had permanently expelled four students.

It was now time for me to zero in on those staff members who were not fulfilling the needs of our students. This included everyone – custodians, teaching staff, security, substitute teachers, assistants to the teachers, and the administration staff. From the very first staff meeting, I admitted to everyone that I'd made both bad mistakes and good changes over the years.

I expressed my passion for our students and my desire to change the image and culture of this school. I specifically said, "I am on a mission. I want this school to be the best—not second best." I gave everyone an opportunity to grow with me, and I offered support to those who might have been out of touch or had lost connectivity with their students, and forgotten their visions and purposes. I regularly walked into classrooms unannounced to see which teacher needed support and who was reading the daily newspaper, on the computer looking at the stock market report or ordering something on eBay. I would conference with them along with their union representative and ask, "We have a tough job to do. How can you do it if you're not making your students a priority?"

Those who resisted change began to give me a bad rap in the staff lounge as they looked for supporters. As the social climate had changed, public schools were under scrutiny more than ever, and business as usual could not—and would not—continue on my watch. I knew it would be a tedious and thankless job to help those teachers who would not work for the betterment of their students. However, I was being forced into being a catalyst to help them decide whether to continue what they had done or accepting the help I offered them so that they could become renewed teachers and role models.

They had to make that decision. I couldn't do it for them. I could only suggest this to them. If they didn't want to change, they had two choices. One was that they could request a transfer to another school in the district. Another, they could retire. They were aware of the consequences (of being fired) if they chose to stay in the building and refused to make improvements in their classrooms and teaching methods. And I continued to require improvement.

During my tenure as the principal and director, there were a few staff members who chose to be resistant and maintain their own agendas. I would not tolerate this. My vision was to have a well-organized school and a team of professionals who loved to teach and were excellent role models for our students. I was their coach, and at the end of the school year, I wanted our school to be in first place.

During our first year, we had laid down the foundation and sent a clear message to the student body and staff that the bar would be raised even further as I continued to fine-tune the culture of our school. "Mediocrity will not be the norm anymore," I told the staff in my closing comments when we prepared to leave for the summer break. I couldn't wait for the next school year to begin.

The Counselor Julie

Over the years, I had witnessed counselors whose visions were very different from the typical description of a high-school counselor. Their job definition read something like this: "School counselors assist students at all levels, from elementary school to college. They act as advocates for students' well-being and as valuable resources for their educational advancement. On the job, school counselors should listen to students' concerns about academic, emotional, or social problems."

In the beginning of my first year as principal, the counselor who was assigned to our building left for another school in the district. I took it personally. She had heard how I felt and said "That if you loved being with the students, you will be a player on my team. If not, you would have to change your thinking or transfer out of the building".

Transferring out of a school was not easy. There were many hoops to jump through, interviews with the administration teams, district seniority, qualifications, and so on. Over the years, I sat in numerous meetings with counselors who really were sincere and devoted to ensuring

248

the best for their students. Unfortunately, they were the minority, not the majority. Counselors were to assist any student who needed an advocate, to act as valuable resources for the students and to listen to their concerns. In other words, assist any student who needed guidance in learning and succeeding in school.

A frustrated teacher might seek out a school counselor to help understand a student who had a discipline issue, was failing academically, and had personal problems that affected his or her learning or was coming to school disheveled.

A number of years earlier, I had issues with one of my seniors. He was constantly late for class and in jeopardy of failing my program and not graduating. I made many phone calls to his home to request a parent conference about his future, but didn't receive any response. I normally didn't go to the counselor about issues with any of my students unless my back was up against the wall and I had no other alternative. This time I needed her help.

After class was dismissed one day, I went to the main office to speak with the counselor. I knocked on the door, she opened it and said, "Come on in, Frank. I will be right with you." Her desk was clean and neat, not a piece of paper in sight. I did notice the current issue of *Cosmopolitan* sitting on the far right of the desk and the fresh smell of hair spray in the air. There was also a handheld mirror on the left side of the desk. I overheard her saying on the phone, "I will be there in a few minutes. Reserve a table for me." She finished and turned to me. "What can I do for you, Frank?"

"Do you have any information regarding the student in my class who might not graduate?"

"What student are you referring to?"

"I have sent you two referrals regarding this kid. He is tardy and truant from my program. I have made several attempts to contact his parents, and I can't connect with them. I never receive any acknowledgment of my phone calls. I need some help from you."

"I will get back to you soon. Is there anything else you want to discuss with me?"

"No."

"OK, talk to you later."

I was extremely pissed off with her response, but didn't want to display my negative and frustrated attitude. After all, in the eyes of the administration team, she was number one. Her reputation hinged on working with those students who were college bound and to place them into top-notch universities. The counselor didn't want to rock the boat and work with those who were work bound or on the edge of failing. She probably thought let's sweep those kids under the table and pretend they are not in our school.

I went back to my classroom and prepared for the next class. She never did get back with me. A few weeks later, as graduation was nearing, the counselor placed a form in our mailbox to fill out for any students who were in jeopardy of not graduating. The district had to keep a file to support the reasons why a student would not be graduating. I submitted this student's name, the one I had been trying to get help with. I noted that I hadn't received the support that I had repeatedly requested from the sending school counselor or the counselor in our building.

Then, suddenly everyone became alarmed and wanted to cover their asses. They were *now* interested in helping this student graduate. I wasn't surprised. They all knew I maintained complete records on every student and documented every time I made phone calls to the parents and contacted and communicated with the counselors—written and verbal. This included conferencing with the student in an attempt to improve attendance in my program. I had all of my bases covered with documentation.

A meeting was scheduled for the two counselors, the student and his parents and me. I couldn't wait to find out why I could never make contact with the parents.

I walked into the conference room with an attitude, but I maintained a smile on my face. I didn't see the student or his home-school counselor. However, I did see a young lady who appeared to be in her mid-twenties. She was dressed in a business suit. I discovered she was the student's sister. Again, I said to myself, "Where are his parents? Where is the student and the home-school counselor?" We waited…

Approximately fifteen minutes after the meeting was scheduled to begin, the conference room door opened, and my student and his counselor walked into the room. The counselor was dressed to the nines, hair and makeup perfect. My student was dressed as I had never seen him before. He was a carbon copy of John Travolta in the movie *Saturday Night Fever*. He looked as if he had just gotten out of the shower. His hair was shiny and still wet.

I said to the student, "You continue to dig yourself into a hole. Why are you late?"

His counselor said, "Oh, it's not his fault. It's mine. I was late picking him up from his house this morning."

I said, "You did what?"

"He didn't have a ride to school, so I decided to pick him up from his home."

"Where are your parents?" The room was silent. You could have heard a pin drop. I said again, "Where are your parents?"

His sister said, "They moved to another state."

I asked, "Who do you live with?"

They answered at the same time. His sister said, "He lives with me." And he said, "I am living alone in my parents' home." The school counselor's face was beet red.

I couldn't restrain myself any longer. I said in a loud firm voice, "What's going on here? Someone is trying to slip me the big green weenie!"

They were shocked at my words, and I could see the expressions on their faces as they kept themselves from bursting out laughing. Everyone knew what I was referring to. These "helpful" people were trying to make it appear as if they were working in the best interests of the student. That this was a cover-up was as clear as their red faces.

Here was an eighteen-year-old student living at home without supervision and a female counselor covering for his attendance—and shitting a brick that this kid would not graduate. I held all of the cards, and everyone knew it. This wasn't a good situation for anyone, especially for the student.

"Well, Mr. A. What will need to happen for him to pass your class and graduate?"

I drew up a contract for the student that he was required to follow to be able to walk across that stage and receive his high-school diploma. He was a good kid, but I wasn't about to compromise the integrity of my program because of his lack of supervision and inappropriate behavior.

It had not been that long ago that I was in his shoes. We were the same way when we were growing up—we will get away with whatever we can as long as we do not get caught. This kid was suffering from a total absence of adult supervision, and no one was holding him accountable for his actions.

The next day in my class, I overheard him talking to his classmates about how close he came to not graduating. He asked to talk to me privately in my office and He said with a smile, "Thank you, Mr. A., for giving me a second chance."

I said to him, "I was a young and single man at one time, and although I do not condone what appears to be going on, I understand it. Now get back in the shop and focus on graduation, not on your testosterone."

Now that I was a principal, I knew my school needed a counselor who truly cared. My staff and I set up a process for the interviews. When the district posted the opening for a counselor to be assigned to our school, and the process of reviewing the applicants and arranging the individual interviews was all set, I said to myself, "Let the interviews begin."

One at a time, the interview committee asked the candidates questions related to the position. We created scenarios describing students who might be in jeopardy of failing, who were hurting themselves, or who were being bullied. The answers we heard in response to our scenarios were unbelievable. The candidates' responses were not what we wanted to hear by a long shot.

For example, I asked one candidate, "A student is being bullied in the classroom and comes to you with this problem. How you will address this?"

The candidate answered, "How will I address this? Is this happening during school or on the bus? I believe I would recommend that the parents take the student to a private outside counselor."

I said, "OK, thank you for your time. We will get back to you in a few days." No way would I consider having that counselor in my school. Next, please.

The next candidate was concerned about dismissal time and whether the counselor's responsibility would extend to after-school activities. Next, please.

For the next candidate, I addressed the formal and informal questions pertaining to the position, and everything seemed to be going smoothly until I gave the candidate another scenario. Oh my God, I couldn't believe the response.

I said to the interviewee, "Here is a scenario, and I want to know how you would react and what you would do in this situation. A student is having gender-identity issues and contemplating suicide. The student comes into your office two minutes before the dismissal bell is ready to ring. How would you address this immediate issue?"

"I would explain to the student how I can be of assistance and provide him with alternative solutions. Then, I'd explain that I had a tennis tournament today and can't be late. Here is a pass to come down to my office tomorrow, and we can we talk about this. I may be able to recommend a psychiatrist whom you can see."

"Thank you," I managed to get out. "I will get back to you."

I said to the team, "We have one more person to interview, and I know she is coming to us with an elementary-school background. Let's a take a look at her and see what happens."

As soon as she introduced herself, I could tell she was a nurturing, kind, warmhearted counselor. I couldn't be biased. I had to grill and drill her the same way we had the previous candidates. I couldn't deviate because the previous candidates were secondary certified, and this candidate was only elementary and middle-school certified. I couldn't show favoritism to anyone. Throughout the routine interview questions, her responses came from her heart. We saw that in the expression on her face. She had a genuine passion for helping kids.

"OK, let's see how well she does with the scenarios," I said to myself. Then I asked her, "A student comes into your office and tells you bullying is taking place on the school bus and in the classroom. What will you do?"

"Oh my God, that is a bad thing that is happening to our children! I can't believe these kids are doing this to one another." She gave me a fast plan of action. "I will talk with the student, assuring the student that she or he can share this issue with complete confidentiality and trust. I will gather names and inform her that the administration will ensure her safety and protect her. I will talk to the perpetrators and investigate the facts, and I will take the necessary precautions to prevent this happening again. I will design and teach mini peer-mediation classes to teach the students that being bullied or bullying someone is not acceptable." This candidate went on and on and expanded on the many tools that she would use to defuse this type of behavior.

I gave her another scenario, "A student comes into your office three minutes before the dismissal bell is ready to ring and says she is suicidal and needs to talk to you. What will you do?"

She said, "I don't have a set time to leave the building. Students are first. Suicide is the number-one cause of death among teenagers today, and it appears there may be an epidemic. We will never know if and when the thought of killing themselves will actually take place. My job as their counselor is to talk to them and assure them that there are alternative solutions. Many of these kids just need or want someone to talk to and someone who will listen to them. That's my job," she said in a territorial tone of voice. "I am their counselor."

I said to the team, "Does anyone have any questions for her?" They shook their heads, no. I said to the candidate, "Do you have any further questions for me?"

She said with a smile, "No, and I hope I am the person who will be your next counselor."

I said, "I will be getting back to you soon. Do you know the way to the front door?"

"Yes. Good-bye."

"Well, team, what do you think?"

"Mr. A., she is the one! She is the one we are looking for to be our next counselor at this school. Hire her."

I agreed with the team. She was the real deal, and she clearly cared about helping our kids here at the CPC.

The next morning, I filled out the paper work and made the phone call to her. I said, "Good morning. Are you ready to work for me and our team?"

"Yes, I am excited to work for you! I can't wait!"

"See you in a few days."

We now had a major-league counselor on our team, and I could feel it in the air—our school had no way to go but up. We would make history.

Meeting in My Office

The new counselor (Julie) had moved into her office and was given a warm welcome from the staff. I said to her, "Will you meet me in my office when you have the time?"

She said with a serious look on her face, "Is everything all right, Mr. A.?"

"Oh, yes, there's no problem. I want to discuss a couple of things with you; nothing major."

A little while later, I was talking on the phone with my office door closed, and I heard a knocking on my door. I ended my phone call and said, "Come on in."

"Is this a good time for you?" our new counselor asked.

"Absolutely. Please come in and close the door." I began to express how happy I was to have her as our counselor, and then I shared a few important concerns I had about the student body and how important it would be to keep me posted about what was going on with the students and in their classrooms.

I said, "I want to be kept in the loop at all times. I truly want you to be our counselor and not a scheduler and a college-placement director for those students who are above the norm. I realize scheduling and college placement is a part of being a counselor, but these students are in need of the bigger picture—someone who will listen and guide them through the most critical times of their lives. I want to know everything and every problem these students share with you. I don't mean I want you to break confidentiality about any problems students may be experiencing in their personal, private lives. But anything about the school or school day, I want to know. Do you understand what I mean?"

She smiled and said, "I did some checking up on you too, Mr. A., and I know how strongly you feel about these students. You really care about them, and I am excited to be working here too."

"Great. Is there anything that you will need to kick off the school year?"

"I would like to visit each of the classrooms and introduce myself to the students. Will this be OK with you?"

"Absolutely," I said with a smile as broad as the Brooklyn Bridge. "Great idea. I am in agreement."

She said, "What will the teachers say?"

"Don't worry about the teachers. They will love you for doing this. Even so, I will give them a heads-up that you will be scheduling times and dates for visits."

We were off to a good start this year. I ran through my mental checklist of things I'd had to do:

- Communicate my vision and expectations to my staff. CHECK.
- Hire a counselor who loves kids. CHECK.
- Implement consistent consequences for those students who want to run the school their way and become discipline issues. CHECK.

Our school was on the way to becoming a first-class technical high school. Soon the staff began to arrive earlier than their scheduled times. I witnessed them communicating in the halls and greeting the students as they arrived. This was a sight to see. The school culture was beginning to change slowly and for the right reasons. My management style was infectious, and it was beginning to rub off on everyone. I was also at peace knowing these kids would have an excellent counselor to go to for any reason. Now it was time to move on to other areas that needed to be fine-tuned.

First Appearances

I was and still am an old school thinker. When I was growing up, men wore suits, and women wore dresses. Oh, I know the times have changed. However, even the teachers wore whatever they wanted and deemed that acceptable. The students dressed even more differently than I was accustomed to.

Despite the changing times, I decided the principal and staff needed to set an example of professionalism. Somehow, someone had approved a dress-code exception called "Casual Fridays." What the hell? Casual Fridays? I didn't say much. I kept my opinions to myself and went along with the flow. Not all staff dressed as if they were going to a rock concert. Some continued to dress business casual and in a professional manner. I wore a dark business suit and tie every day except on Casual Fridays. On those days, I wore business-casual attire in order to fit in.

I believed the first impression we made in our classrooms and with the people we saw every day was important. The clothes we wore were important to establish a professional front to other people. In other words, if we were to be respected, we had to dress and act the part. We had to be professional.

On occasion I would make an announcement over the school public-address system, reminding the boys and girls about their fashion choices. "Good morning, staff and students. I want to remind our students that you are not attending a nightclub. This is school. I am asking you to dress moderately and appropriately for school. Teachers, I am asking you to note those students who continue to dress inappropriately and refuse to adhere to my request. Please send them to my office. Students, we will continue to maintain a school culture that will make everyone take note and want to imitate. Please cooperate with me. I thank you, and have a great day."

My message was not intended to be intimidating, but I wanted these kids to be aware we were going to run a school that would reflect professionalism, teaching them through example to enter the real working world. There would be rules they would have to learn and follow. They might not like it, but this was the way it would be. Slowly, most of the students complied. However, some refused, and therefore, I stepped it up. The girls were sent to a female for review, and the boys…well, let me share what I did with the boys who refused to comply.

The boys were wearing their jeans down to their backsides, exposing their underpants. I'd tell them, "Pull up those pants. I don't want to see your underpants." One morning, before I came into the office, I stopped by an all-night department store and purchased all of the belts and suspenders they had on the rack. When I reached the cashier, she asked, "Why are you purchasing all of these belts and suspenders?"

I said, "I am sick and tired of telling the boys in my building to pull up their pants. I'm going to change that."

All the customers behind me in line started to clap, cheering me on and sharing their approval. I headed to school with the new accessories. Those boys who chose to continue to wear their jeans in an inappropriate fashion were in for a surprise. I asked the staff to join me for a brief staff meeting before the students began classes.

"Good morning, staff. If you see any boys who continue to wear their jeans in an inappropriate manner, kindly send them to the office with a written referral. We cannot continue to let the student's control this building or we will be on the losing end. I'm not asking you to start a war with our student body, but I will not have our students running the building. I want to have an equal balance. I am asking for your support. I made a few purchases this morning for those with baggy trousers." I showed them the new accessories I had purchased for the boys, proudly holding them up for all to see.

The staff clapped and smiled, saying, "Go get them, Mr. A."

"Will do!" I said. "Have a good day."

The first student was in my office approximately fifteen minutes after the bell rang.

"Good morning, Mr. A. I have a student referral for you" the secretary said.

"Regarding?"

"His pants."

"Send him in." The student came in. "Please sit down. Is your mom or dad home?"

"Why do you ask?"

"How many times have you been warned to not wear your pants down to your knees?"

"Uh, many."

"Do you think I am fooling around here?"

"Uh, I don't know."

"You don't know?" I said in a loud, clear voice. "How old are you?"

"Almost eighteen years old."

"And you can't follow directions? You are about to be suspended for not following the rules. I would be embarrassed to be a senior in high school, almost eighteen years old, and sent home because I decided not to pull up my pants."

Suddenly I heard a knock on my door. "Everything OK, Mr. A.?"

"Yes, come in."

It was the counselor. "What's going on with this student?"

I said to the student, "Please explain to our counselor the reason you are here."

He began to explain. "I didn't follow the school policy. I'm about to be suspended."

I said to him, "I will give you a choice. The decision will be entirely up to you. I can suspend you for two days and ask your parents to leave their places of work and come to school to pick you up—or you can lease a belt or a pair of suspenders from me. Which choice will you be making this morning?"

"Mr. A., I choose to lease a belt and not be suspended."

"Great choice. Walk over and see the bookkeeper to work out the details. Be sure to return the belt at the end of the year, and you will receive a full refund. I do not want to see you in my office again for not wearing a belt. Am I making myself clear?"

"Yes, Mr. A."

Within a few days, the word was out, and the message was clear: pull up your pants, or Mr. A. will suspend you. Our boys were becoming young men, and they understood my message loud and clear. Many times we learn by example—or from someone who's been made an example of.

Now it was time to address those staff who hadn't complied with my request that they dress in a professional manner. Our staff members were unique in that they all had specialty certifications in the fields that they were teaching. There were twenty-one different programs offered to our students, such as classes in the legal and medical professions, auto-body repair, construction, and culinary arts. Many of our staff members had similar backgrounds to me. They were hired right out of industry and were experts in their chosen fields. Therefore, their personalities were also unique.

Most of the staff had conformed to my recommendations by wearing the appropriate clothing for the classes they were teaching. Here are a few examples. Teachers in our legal and medical programs dressed in business casual. The culinary arts teacher wore a clean, appropriate chef's uniform, and the building trades teacher dressed accordingly. I would often remind the staff, "If you want respect and a well-organized classroom, this all begins with the teacher. If your appearance is professional, your students will follow and emulate you. Please think about their perception of you."

On occasion, I would send out a friendly memo to remind the staff that "Casual Fridays occur at the end of the week, not on Tuesdays or any other day week." Most understood, some thought I was being humorous, but everyone complied except one staff member who continued to dress unprofessionally and maintained the appearance of a homeless person. This drove me up a wall, and I believe he knew it. I went to his colleagues and asked for their assistance. I said to them, "Will you please persuade that teacher to follow the program and dress appropriately so he can be a good role model to the students in the class?"

They said, "Mr. A., we have made many suggestions and asked the teacher to comply with your requests. He just laughs in our faces."

I said, "OK, I will take care of this. Thanks for trying to help me with this awkward situation."

I went back to my office and contacted the president of the teachers union. I told him about the situation. The president said, "It's unfortunate that a few staff members want to challenge the role of the administrator. Frank, what you are asking of this person is reasonable. I visit all of the buildings periodically throughout the district, and most of the staff dress in a professional manner. However, there are some who come to work like they just rolled out of bed. I agree that this creates a negative atmosphere in the classroom. Sometimes teachers tell me that they do not have any classroom respect or control, and I want to say, 'Take a look in the mirror before you leave your house in the morning.'"

I said, "Can I legally send this teacher home to change and clean up his appearance without any repercussions?"

"Yes, although you will be the first administrator I have worked with in the past thirty years to actually do it."

"OK, thanks for the information. I didn't want to overstep my bounds."

"Frank, when the word gets out to the rank and file, you will be sending a clear message to those who do not want to comply with the district. As teachers, we are professionals, and we need to act like professionals too."

I confirmed this with human resources, and they too agreed with my decision and said, "Frank, you have a set of giant balls to do this. Good luck. We will support your decision here in the central office."

"Thank you for your support." I immediately left my office, walked down the long hallway to the classroom and knocked on the teacher's door. The teacher greeted me. "Yes, Mr. A. Can I help you?"

I said, "Yes, you can. I have sent you memos and given you several warnings regarding your personal appearance, and you have continually refused to make an attempt to clean up your act. I am dismissing you, effective immediately, to go home, take a shower, change your clothes, and return to school tomorrow dressed like a professional. Do I make myself clear?"

The teacher was at a loss for words but finally said, "You can't do this! I am calling the union president. I will file a grievance on you!"

I replied, "I covered all of my bases, and I have the right to do this. I have exhausted every avenue I could think of trying to persuade you to dress like a professional. Now get out of the building."

Whoa. That day's event went through the gossip and rumor mill as if someone had poured gasoline on a dried-out Christmas tree. I didn't want to do this to a staff member, but other teachers were putting pressure on me to make a decision to do something. Our building was stepping up a notch, and other staff continued to adjust and support the decisions from the main office. Our counselor continued to keep me in the loop, doing exactly what I had hoped she would be doing.

One day she sheepishly came into my office and said, "Can I talk to you?"

"Yes. What's going on Julie? I can see by the expression on your face that something is wrong."

She said, "Remember you said to me that you wanted to know everything that is going on in the building regarding our students?"

"Please tell me what's wrong."

She began to say, "I have a female student in my office crying. She will not go back to her classroom." She paused and asked me, "Are you all right, Mr. A.?"

"Yes, why do you ask?"

"Your eyes look like they're going to pop out of the sockets."

My blood had begun to boil, and I could feel my eye sockets beginning to stretch beyond their limits. "Tell me what's going on."

"There's a teacher who has a sign posted in his room that says, "SMART PEOPLE DO IT ONCE. STUPID PEOPLE DO IT TWICE.""

I immediately jumped out of my seat and walked down to this classroom to see where this sign was posted for myself. After entering the classroom, I received a friendly welcome from the students. "Good morning, Mr. A."

As I walked about the classroom, the teacher also said to me, "Good morning, Mr. A. Can I help you?" I didn't answer him. I was on a mission. I walked right up to that poster placed clearly in front of his class for all to read. I grabbed the corner and ripped it off the bulletin board, using such force that the thumb tacks went flying all over the classroom. I crumpled up the poster as I said to the teacher, "Please see me after class today."

266

You could hear a pin drop as I left his classroom. I didn't know if it was from fear of me ripping the poster off the board or if the students were happy to see the sign removed. I returned to my office with the sign and said to the counselor, "Those kids will never see that sign again!"

She said, "I've never seen you that angry! I thought your eyes were going to pop out of your head."

"Thank you for bringing this to my attention. I will have to monitor that program more closely. Now I know why enrollment is always low over there." I thanked God that teacher saw the writing on the wall and made a decision to retire at the end of the school year. Good riddance, and don't let the door hit you in the behind.

Infusing Academics into Hands-On Learning

Soon the word was out. Our school was shedding its reputation as a retirement home. However, there were still more challenges and hurdles ahead of us. The pressure was on from the Department of Education at the state and federal levels about raising the graduation requirements. These new requirements would have a direct impact on incoming students interested in attending our school within the next two years. Career and technical education already had mathematics and science infused into the curriculum, but the students couldn't receive credit for the academic component because these subjects didn't meet the guidelines as outlined by the Department of Education.

We had to move fast. Many obstacles were in our way, and there was a tremendous amount of work ahead of us. We were facing low enrollment, and now we had to handle the infusion of math and science into the curriculum so that our classes would fulfill the mandated credits for high-school graduation. Although these requirements would not affect us for two years, we had to move fast or we would be closed down. The district could justify closing our school permanently without any repercussions from the community or the bargaining units. This would be a serious situation for everyone, if this building were to be closed. It wouldn't be on my watch! Not a chance I'd let this happen. I was a fighter, and I knew how important it was to continue programs that our kids needed and that would endure long after I retired and sailed into the sunset.

As soon as I received all of the facts and details about the new curriculum, I scheduled a staff meeting and outlined the consequences. I said to the staff that we needed their cooperation 100 percent.

This meeting was to shake and wake everyone up, and I didn't hold back from telling it like it was. "If the district makes a decision to close our building because we cannot meet the new curriculum guidelines, it will be too late for you to modify your courses. Now is the time we need to start this, not in two years. If we're closed, some of you will be reassigned to other buildings to teach other subjects. Those of you whose certifications are in vocational education will most likely be surplus, which means you will lose your jobs. It's that simple.

"As you are aware, curriculum is not my expertise, and therefore I am asking you to help me with this monumental task and step up to the plate. I need your help. Some will have more to do than others, but I am asking for a 100 percent effort from and by everyone. Am I making myself clear?"

This was a time for the staff to set aside all their biases and issues with me, the students, and the district. We didn't have time for mind games. It was do or die for our school.

I contacted a small group of retired teachers with whom I had developed an excellent rapport over the years, and I asked them for their help with our curriculum. My assistant principal was very knowledgeable about curriculum matters, and she knew how to cross the T's and dot the I's. She stepped up and led the committee, and I took care of the needs of the group. We all spent many hours working on the content and attending meetings, but in the end, the committee pulled together the substantial amount of documentation requested by the state and district. It was now time to present our curriculum infused with math and science to the school board for approval.

Prior to the board meeting, I took everyone out to dinner and thanked them for their hard work. I knew upon approval, this would be a win-win for everyone. Our school enrollment would flourish and increase, and the district would be famous for having the first career technical school in the state of Michigan to offer math and science credits within traditional hands-on programs.

I asked the staff to be present for the board meeting that evening to show solidarity and unity. All of us being visible would give the school-board members a message that we were not going away. I made the introductions, stating our purpose along with a brief overview. I then asked our assistant principal to come up and begin the PowerPoint presentation, outlining in detail our proposal to infuse math and science into our programs. Sitting in my seat, I observed the board members smiling and nodding their heads in agreement. The assistant principal's presentation ended, and she asked, "Members of the board, can I answer any questions you may have?"

The room was quiet. We could hear some whispering going on among the board members. Soon, the board secretary announced, "We will now vote on the approval of curriculum infusion of math and science in the courses offered at the CPC."

As each board member's name was called, all I heard was "Approve. Approve. Approve." I was as proud as a new father that night.

That evening, the board unanimously approved the curriculum changes at the CPC. The staff and the audience clapped and cheered for us. We were now at the forefront of career and technical education.

The next day, the feeling of pride and confidence among our staff was at an all-time high. Once again, I scheduled a staff meeting and congratulated the staff for their victory. I thanked them all for stepping up and digging in deep for these outstanding programs—and for the future of our school. I will never forget that night.

We were off and running once again. Optimism was in the air.

Student Awards and Recognition

As I have said so many times before, the majority of our students were not the type who received recognition for their outstanding accomplishments in sports or academics. They were just average students. But these kids were great, and they needed to be recognized for being great kids. I was as proud of them as their parents were.

I recalled the days participating in the Autorama, and I knew how much pride and self-esteem these kids received from winning those competitions. I'd watch them with a tear in my eye as they walked up and received the trophy for all of their hard work and the many long hours they'd spent building our award-winning show cars.

Now, I wanted all of the students in my school to experience that moment of joy as they walked across the stage with their parents in the audience able to see their success.

Therefore, I implemented a student-award night, giving their teachers an opportunity to share with the audience the students' improvements and the positive contributions they had made in the classroom. Earlier on in the school year, I proposed the idea in another one of my staff meetings. I asked our staff, "Do you have any thoughts about hosting an awards night for our student body?"

Some of the staff frowned at the idea because this would be added work in their already overloaded schedules. However, after everyone had the time to consider my proposal, I received their approval and support.

The counselor and the administration team would spearhead this project. I assured the staff they would have a minimal amount of additional work, and the secretarial and administrative staff would be carrying the greatest portion of the load. I didn't want this to become a burden, but the teachers were key to making this event a success. No one knew the students as well as their teachers.

Our commercial art department designed the certificates, and the print shop program printed them out. Printed on each certificate were the student's name and the class he or she was in. The school logo added a special flair. We also designed and printed a program that included a list of guest dignitaries from the district. Our guest speaker was an alumnus who gave a testimonial and encouraged our kids not to give up on their dreams and to set goals they could attain. It was a night to remember.

I received many congratulatory cards from the staff, students, and parents praising the school for hosting this great event. The awards quickly became an annual celebration. I was big on promoting our school, programs, and staff. Soon the word was out, and enrollment grew. We were no longer referred to as a "retirement home" or a "country club." Promote, promote, and promote some more—this was what our school needed, and I was the person to do it. Every time the students won awards or were doing something innovative in the classroom, I contacted our local newspapers and television stations. The CPC was now a buzzword around the tri-county area. Everyone knew or had heard about the CPC.

Soon I would be facing another challenge.

Remodeling

The CPC first opened in the fall of September 1975. Although the school was basically in good shape, the building was thirty-two years old and needed modifications and classroom upgrades. As the building principal, once again I scheduled a staff meeting. I told our staff the district's plans and scope for remodeling the building. I also asked the staff for their individual classroom needs, including their wants and wish lists.

I knew what my priorities would be—updating the ergonomics of the building and making the building more student-friendly. I envisioned a student commons and seating area for the students to enjoy.

I also wanted to give our health-sciences program a physical-therapy room, with the most modern workout equipment for training and exercise purposes. Teaching could be stressful at times, and I wanted the best for our staff. I thought that with such a room at the school, the staff would have an opportunity to exercise daily in their free time. I justified purchasing this equipment because it would be used as part of the curriculum, in the physical-training and rehabilitation segments of the program. My real motive for purchasing this equipment was simple. I wanted it for our staff to use.

All three high schools in the district had workout rooms that were second to none, and they were all accessible for their staff members to use. The CPC was excluded from this opportunity because we did not have an athletic program. Being a leader means providing a great working environment for the staff too.

The construction and renovation on our building meant organized chaos, but luckily, only for a short period of time. The teachers had ample time to remove their personal items and pack away their classroom supplies and equipment during the last two weeks of that school year. There were stressful and rushed moments, but we all survived. In the fall of the new school year, the dust had settled and we were all ready to move back into our renovated school. There was excitement in the air, for we couldn't wait to see our newly remodeled building.

I walked through the front door, and there it was—a new student commons area, a place to sit and enjoy, a place where they would be able discuss their daily lessons, have a snack, and enjoy their school. Students needed to connect with one another, and they needed to feel that this was their school too.

The culture of our school had changed dramatically in the past four years. Enrollment had increased. The building had been renovated. Technology had been improved. The staff who weren't interested in helping and providing for our students had retired. The students enrolled in our programs for the wrong reasons were no longer enrolled. All our students understood that we believed in them and wanted to give them the best possible education that we could. As planned, our school was becoming a first-class operation, and everyone knew it.

Enrollment continued to grow, and for most classes, there was a waiting list. Life was going great for our school as we continuously investigated programs and ways of improving our curriculums. Our assistant principal attended statewide workshops and conferences on a regular basis. She evaluated the current trends in the industry and looked into ways to infuse these trends into the current curriculum of our programs. We worked to ensure that our school would stay ahead of everyone else. We were pioneers at implementing new and valuable course offerings for our students. We wanted our graduating students who chose to attend the CPC on the cutting edge and ready for success.

A New Governor

2009

The election of a new governor was nearing and I faced an especially difficult challenge. The candidates who put their hats into the ring were narrowed down to the final two.

One candidate was the former mayor of a large town near our state capital, and the other was a successful businessman whose platform was based on reducing out-of-control spending and bringing jobs back to Michigan. There was a liberal candidate and a conservative. The liberals would spend, and the conservatives would not. Some of our automotive and related businesses had left the state, and the state had to spend monies it didn't have. Our financial deficit grew as Michigan slid deeper into debt.

A rumor circulated that employees were going to be offered incentives to retire. Here's part of an article explaining that offer.

"State Employees Consider Early Retirement"

by Jamie Edmonds

Just like thousands of teachers did months ago, state employees now have a decision to make: stay or go.

"There's a carrot and stick with this bill," Mitch Bean, director of the House Fiscal agency, said.

Last week, the legislature passed an almost identical retirement incentive package for state workers as they did for Michigan's teachers back in June. Basically, the plan offers a larger group the opportunity to retire.

"There are two sets of folks eligible," Bean said. "Those currently eligible to retire under the current system, and those that are now eligible under the new incentive plan."

Under the current system: someone who is either 60 years old with 10 years or more of experience, or someone who is 55 years old with 30 years or more experience can retire with a 1.6 percent multiplier.

Anyone who has 30 years of experience, regardless of age, plus years of work equals 80, is eligible at a 1.55 multiplier.

"State employees' pensions are not nearly as much as people think they are," Bean said. "It's only $22,000–$23,000 per year. With this incentive, that would be increased by 6 percent."

Which on average, Bean said, would equal out to an extra $1,500 to $2,000 more per year in retirement for those who take the offer.

About 3,500 state employees are eligible under this retirement incentive, but they don't have much time to think about it. A decision must be made by early November.18

I faced the choice of retiring at the age of sixty. I didn't want to retire. I loved my job, and I loved what I was doing—making a difference in our schools and helping our kids become successful. I was at the top of my game and my career, but my focus for the past thirty-five years could soon be coming to an end. I needed to make a decision, and I

---

[18] Posted September 30, 2010, on
http://www.wilx.com/home/headlines/104109703.html

needed to do it quickly. As soon as I knew the retirement incentives would be a one-time offering, my stomach began to turn. Rolaids didn't help much.

This would be another decision for Chris and I to face. Retiring would be a whole new phase of our lives. Many thoughts and what-ifs came into the picture. Most of all, I wasn't ready to retire, but if I chose to stay on and work, my retirement compensation and benefits would actually be less when I retired in the future.

I opted to retire.

I made the decision to retire at the end of the 2009–2010 school year. My announcement came as a surprise for many because of my age. However, the people whom I loved the most were excited to see me retire and begin to enjoy a new phase of life with my family. After the parties ended and the congratulations cards were read and filed away, the reality of being retired began to sink in.

Chris and I had to adjust to my reduced income and rely on our investments and our savings to supplement our lifestyle. This sounds easy, but believe me, we had an adjustment phase to go through. I kept saying to myself, "There is never enough money, never enough time, and want, want, want. How much and how many material things do I really need?"

-0-

I have been truly blessed. Christine and I have been married for forty-six years, raised three children, have five grandchildren, and a beautiful home—and there's a garage filled with cool cars! How much more do I need? How much do I want? How long will I live?

Oh yes, I almost forgot. I am reminded by God that these were given to me from him and are on loan to me. I will not be taking any of them with me when I am called to be with him. Having the most has now taken a back seat in my life. It is now time to become reacquainted with and grow closer to my loving wife.

To be continued…

Made in the USA
Columbia, SC
17 March 2023

13756245R00161